MAKING FOREIGN POLICY

Making Foreign Policy

Policy

A Certain Idea of Britain

JOHN COLES

JOHN MURRAY
Albemarle Street, London

© John Coles 2000

First published in 2000
by John Murray (Publishers) Ltd,
50 Albemarle Street, London W1X 4BD

The moral right of the author has been asserted

A catalogue record for this book is available from the British Library

ISBN 0-7195-6046-2

Typeset in 12/14pt Bembo by Servis Filmsetting Ltd, Manchester

Printed and bound in Great Britain by the University Press Cambridge

FOR ANNE
*With gratitude for her support
in my career and in
admiration of her own
achievements*

CONTENTS

PREFACE

This book is about policy-making, in particular the process of making British foreign policy. In November 1997, after a diplomatic career of thirty-seven years, I retired from the posts of Permanent Under-Secretary at the Foreign and Commonwealth Office and Head of the Diplomatic Service. For some time, and particularly in my last years of service, I had become increasingly concerned that the capacity of the Foreign Office* and of government more widely to make policy had declined. Some of the causes seemed clear. Policy-making, by which I mean the formulation of a course of action (or sometimes a statement of attitude) to deal with a situation or problem, did not command the same priority as in earlier years. For a decade or more governments had placed increasing emphasis on management. They

---

*Throughout I use the abbreviated terms 'Foreign Office' and 'Foreign Secretary' instead of the more correct 'Foreign and Commonwealth Office' and 'Secretary of State for Foreign and Commonwealth Affairs' which would weary by endless repetition.

had looked to senior civil servants to devote more of their time to management, to develop and apply new management techniques, some adopted from the private sector. Increasingly, officials were judged by their ability to manage their budgets and staff efficiently, to make financial savings and to respond positively to new managerial requirements imposed from the centre of government.

Over about the same period another new priority had emerged: presentation. Of course, the need to present policy is nearly as old as policy itself. But in recent years the time and effort devoted to presentation – to Parliament, to public opinion, and, critically, to the media – had grown exponentially. This requirement could and often did take up several hours in the working day of a minister. Officials responded to the same demand. Presentation came to be regarded as an integral part of policy-making. Indeed, it sometimes seemed that presentation drove policy, that the need to describe, explain and defend influenced, almost dictated, the very substance of policy.

But there were other factors at work too. The sheer complexity of modern government, the speed of communications, the extraordinary growth in the quantity of available information, the increased workload imposed on ministers and officials by these and other developments, all tended to limit the time and resources available for policy analysis and formulation. Time spent on management, on presentation, on digesting information, on responding to the day-to-day and often unpredictable demands of government is time lost for policy-thinking, for planning, for the formulation and orderly pursuit of policy objectives.

All the problems I have mentioned affect the making of foreign as well as domestic policy. But international affairs also present special problems for policy-makers. With the best will in the world much foreign policy has to be reactive, a matter of responding to events happening outside Britain. Unpredictability is more dominant in this than in most other areas of government. The task of setting and pursuing clear objectives is therefore harder. Unpredictability aside, successive governments have found it difficult to devise and portray a clear role for Britain overseas, to convey an 'idea of Britain'. Historically, this had much to do with relative economic decline, the need constantly to shift and adapt as economic pressures dictated. It had much to do, also, with ambiguity about Britain's relationship with continental Europe. Whatever one's personal opinion about the desirable nature of that relationship, it is plain that without a settled view of it the task of deciding what Britain should be attempting to do in its foreign policy becomes extremely difficult.

I was not alone in my concern about the quality of policy-making. I became accustomed to the often strongly voiced complaints of both ministers and officials that they simply lacked the time for sufficient thought about policy. Whether it was a matter of planning, of formulating fundamental objectives or of constructing the right policy response to a specific problem or sudden crisis, the time needed for considered thought was often not available. This seemed to me a serious problem that had not received the attention it deserved. I decided, therefore, that I would devote a period of my retirement to reflecting on it in the hope that I could understand it better and perhaps contribute to solutions. I was fortunate enough to be awarded a Visiting Fellowship at All Souls College, Oxford, for two terms in 1998 – which gave me the opportunity and facilities to read, think and write, and I am most grateful to the College for their generosity. For the first time I became aware of the full range of academic and other works that analyse and criticize the defects in policy-making. This was a chastening, if salutary, experience about which I shall have more to say later. But it certainly deepened my understanding of the nature and causes of the problem. I particularly thank Professor Robert O'Neill and Sir Julian Bullard of All Souls College, as well as Sir Percy Cradock, Professor Peter Hennessy, Professor Kathleen Burk and Dr Anne Coles who all read an earlier text and made many helpful suggestions. My thanks are also due to Gail Pirkis, my editor at John Murray, for her skill and professionalism, and to the Library and Records Department of the Foreign Office for valuable help with facts and documents.

This book is written in the conviction that policy matters, indeed in the belief that good policy-making is the heart of good government and that, however unfashionable it may be to say so, management and presentation are, and should be regarded as, secondary and supportive skills. For in the end policy has a far greater influence on the lives of individuals. Good management can save money, bring greater efficiency, produce a more contented and effective workforce. Good presentation undoubtedly helps the implementation of policy and the

acquisition of public support which is increasingly necessary for effective government. But neither can compensate
for the damage done by inadequate or bad policy which,
in its human, financial and other consequences, can be
severely harmful. I have another conviction: policy-
making is hard. It needs intellectual rigour, a capacity for
innovation, a grasp of political reality, a sense of the future
and, quite often, a certain courage. It should, as a function
of government, be put back on its proper pedestal. I find
it encouraging that the present British government have
recently established a Centre for Management and Policy
Studies with a specific role in identifying new policy-
thinking, and that the Prime Minister has publicly stated
that 'We need to ask ourselves searching questions about
policy-making', appealing for a longer-term approach to
decision-making by both ministers and officials, and a less
risk-averse attitude.[1] Mr Blair has called for a public debate
on these issues, to which I hope this book may be a useful
contribution.

In most of what follows I concentrate on the process of
making foreign policy because I am better qualified to deal
with that than with the wider process of policy-making in
Whitehall. But much of the analysis is relevant to domestic policy-making as well. I do not deal with the *substance*
of British foreign policy except in so far as it is inseparable
from the policy-making process or is necessary for the
purposes of illustration. At the outset I acknowledge that
the arguments I advance would benefit from case studies,
from an account of real foreign policy-making episodes.
But examples from the distant past would have little

relevance to the problems of policy-making today. For the more recent period the archives are closed and I am bound by the rules which limit the ability of former Diplomatic Service officers to draw on official information acquired during their careers. Nevertheless, this is not a theoretical study. The analysis and reflection are firmly based on long experience of helping to make policy.

A book which concentrates on the *process* of making policy is open to the charge that what matters is results, not how you get there. I agree that a policy is good or bad in so far as it meets British interests and objectives. But I believe that policy success is much more likely if the process is itself sound.

This is not a work of criticism. One of the advantages of a diplomatic career is that it provides an almost unique opportunity for studying Britain from the perspective of abroad and for comparing the British way with that of others, without the constant distraction of the barrage of anti-government criticism which is the stock-in-trade of so much of our media. That experience, over nearly four decades, has left me with the belief that, for all its faults, our system of government, and the politicians who direct and the civil servants who advise, are in general about as good as you can find anywhere and better than most. Which does not mean that all is well with the state or I would not have written this book.

Beaulieu
September 1999

I

A CASE TO ANSWER?

When working inside government I was only dimly aware of academic and other criticisms of the policy-making process in Britain. I suspect that most of my former civil service colleagues were equally oblivious of them. That was, perhaps, unfortunate. Both the critics and we might have benefited from greater familiarity with each other. The obstacles on our side were not, I think, an unwillingness to expose ourselves to criticism nor a desire to protect 'secrets', for there is little about the policy-making process that need be secret. Our difficulty was largely a matter of available time. We had little enough time for policy-thinking itself let alone for considering at any length the criticisms of outsiders. Only when retirement gave me the leisure to study these was I made aware of how strong and widespread the laments are.

'Britain', writes one academic critic, 'now stands out amongst comparable European countries and perhaps among liberal democracies as a whole, as a state unusually prone to make large-scale, avoidable policy mistakes.'[1] He suggests that policy mistakes on a grand scale are now accepted as inevitable, indeed, almost as routine, and that they are seen as a natural corollary of our system of governing. The most frequently cited example is the introduction of the Poll Tax where, it is argued, the government ignored a great deal of objective advice to the effect that the policy was not capable of implementation, thereby in the event wasting a substantial amount of taxpayers' money. While the burden of the criticism in this case is directed at political misjudgement, the civil service is also held to have been ineffective in its warnings and poor in its policy advice.[2] Many other policies of recent years have also attracted unfavourable comment. The decision, following the 1985 Review of Social Security, to encourage people to opt out of state earnings-related pension schemes and to invest instead in personal pension plans foundered because, on the basis of private sector advice considered to be misleading, people were persuaded to invest in pension plans which were subsequently shown not to offer commensurate benefits. The insurance industry had to provide several billions of pounds in compensation to those who had been misled in this way. Then the decision, in 1993, to establish the Child Support Agency in order to pursue divorced parents who were not contributing to the upkeep of dependent children and to reduce social security costs and remove many single parents from dependence on state benefits failed, it is argued, because of inadequate resources and inflexible and unrealistic rules. The policy had to be substantially reformulated.

In the economic field, many critics cite the 1990 decision to enter the European Exchange Rate Mechanism, followed by forced exit in 1992, as an avoidable and very expensive policy disaster. Some also argue that the 1987–8 recession in the United Kingdom was attributable to policy mistakes which could have been avoided. Other examples discussed in the academic literature are the cumulative erosion of local government in the 1980s, the maintenance of the Trident missile programme after the end of the Cold War, the lack of clear purpose and accountability in the criminal justice system and the ill-fated introduction in 1992 of a new computer system for the dispatch of ambulances by the London Ambulance Service. More recently, the case of BSE has been held to illustrate failures in the policy-making process. No doubt the BSE enquiry, still in progress when this text was completed, will address this issue. The press reports of the enquiry's proceedings already suggest that the episode raises questions about the capacity within government for planning to deal with future contingencies. Finally, outside critics join politicians and others inside government in observing a general decline in the quality of legislation in the 1980s.

Outsiders who were once insiders share at least some of these concerns. 'No one', said Sir Brian Cubbon, a former Permanent Under-Secretary in the Home Office, 'could claim that Government decisions in the last thirty years have been of a high standard.'[3] A former Cabinet Secretary (Lord Hunt of Tanworth) points to the poor quality of policy advice and the need, if not for more advice, then at least for advice given earlier and in greater depth.[4] Sir Peter Kemp, a former Permanent Secretary at the Cabinet Office and Manager of the Next Steps Project, casts doubt on 'competence at the centre' and lists the cases of the Poll Tax, ERM and BSE (among others) as examples of 'policies or policy reactions poorly thought through or poorly carried out or both'.[5] Sir Frank Cooper, Permanent Under-Secretary at the Ministry of Defence from 1976 to 1982, commenting on Mrs Thatcher's period as Prime Minister, states that the Ministry of Defence was left 'leaner, tauter and fitter' by the Thatcherite approach but still with 'remarkably little in the way of defence policy'.[6]

Although some of these cases of alleged policy failure have foreign policy implications I am concerned in this chapter mainly with domestic policy. The record, as portrayed by the critics, is an uncomfortable one. I shall comment on the validity of the criticisms later but first it is worth examining the views of outside observers on the causes of policy failure.

It is an accepted principle of government in Britain that ministers decide what policies should be followed. It is important, therefore, that they should have the time and resources to think about and formulate policy. But for at least three decades ministers have been overloaded. Professor Peter Hennessy, an astute observer of the workings of Whitehall and Westminster, believes the problem is becoming ever more serious.[7] He recalls that as long ago as 1962 Lord Hailsham produced a paper for the then Prime Minister on 'The Machinery of Government', observing that the present system was breaking down. Macmillan reacted to this analysis by putting the problem to Cabinet and telling his ministerial colleagues that the burden on ministers was becoming almost intolerably heavy, not merely in meeting the responsibility of the Cabinet, but also in taking the growing volume of decisions which their departments and the public expected them to take personally, and in facing the daily barrage of the press, radio and television. But neither this nor earlier or later attempts to reduce the burden on ministers had much practical effect. In *The State Under Stress*, Christopher Foster and Francis Plowden assert that the problem has become worse since the end of the 1970s. Alongside the task of policy-making and the preparation of legislation, the number of executive decisions taken by ministers has grown enormously; British membership of the European Community has brought new and growing burdens; the requirement to make speeches and receive deputations has increased; and, most importantly, the demands of the media have become ever more insistent. The same authors believe that the ministerial working day has lengthened in the last thirty years from fourteen to eighteen hours.[8]

If those outside the system identify ministerial overload as a major contemporary problem, those who were inside but are now out would readily agree. Sir Percy Cradock, former Foreign Policy Adviser to the Prime

Minister, writes of 'the almost unsustainable pressure of events and the blizzard of official paper which attempts to record and analyse'. 'Ministers', he continues, 'are governed by diaries which seem designed to break them in physique or spirit in the shortest possible time.'[9] Lord Howe, in his *Memoirs*, puts it even more graphically: 'During six years at the Foreign Office I took home, to work through overnight while others slept, no less than 24 tonnes of paper: three boxes a night, six nights a week, forty weeks a year. Six o'clock was my normal time for getting up. My average bedtime was about four hours earlier.'[10] The consequences for policy-making were obvious to him: 'The problems of overload and of co-ordination are not that the system will fail to work . . . rather that it would work badly, lacking consistency and sufficient thought and analysis.' And the outcome? Hennessy puts it thus: 'The job [of any Cabinet Minister] . . . is a conveyor belt to exhaustion and underachievement all round, a predicament reflected in . . . the finished policy, which is all too often defective and immensely difficult to implement.'[11]

The overburdening of ministers is exacerbated, in the view of external commentators (though it is obvious enough anyway), by the phenomenon of ministerial rotation. The critics of the Poll Tax episode point out that in the eight years it took to devise, introduce and repeal the tax there were seven Secretaries of State for the Environment and under them eight ministers for Local Government.[12] Andrew Marr, whose *Ruling Britannia* has a good deal to say about the shortcomings of our governmental system, finds that the two years which a minister may typically expect to spend in a job are too short a period for policy purposes and observes that 'in the four years covering the biggest shake-up in English schools for a generation, the Education Department had four Secretaries of State'.[13] The impact on government departments of so rapid a succession of ministers is bound to be harmful but there is also the impact on individual ministers to be considered. Lord Howe cites the cases of Sir Leon Brittan, who held three Cabinet jobs in three years, and Kenneth Baker, who had four in seven (with a mere nine months as Secretary of State for the Environment).[14] However able the minister it is probably asking too much to expect well-considered and consistent policy to emerge from a merry-go-round of this kind. Indeed, it results in an in-built bias against consistency since any politician in a senior post will wish to make his or her mark by policy initiatives that can be presented as new. External commentators see the dangers of this. If ministers want media coverage their best bet is to aim for policy change, for 'innovative' policy, because the media may make stories out of what is new but rarely, if ever, out of what is consistent or what is simply the application of well-established policy. In the view of some this leads ministers to take 'endless initiatives to talk up policy change'.[15]

Those involved in the political process are described by the writers just quoted as 'excessively interested in presentation rather than substance, and a sensation-seeking relationship with the media'.[16] But it should not be assumed that all politicians have been willing players in this game. A former Cabinet Minister, Lord Hurd, reflecting after retirement from politics, believed that the burdens placed on ministers by the need to justify their actions to the media were getting out of hand. He judged that after a typical ministerial statement to the House of Commons he could expect to conduct five or six interviews, possibly four for television and two for radio. If he refused, he risked 'critics and commentators filling the gap . . . justification of policy had become as important as its formulation'.[17] The same former minister said in a radio interview: 'Ministers of all Parties fret infinitely about the media. A huge amount of time is given to this fretting. The Cabinet may no longer have to worry about India, but from time to time it worries itself sick about the *Daily Mail*.'

Even some journalists themselves worry about this preoccupation. Magnus Linklater asks whether the present practice of maximum access politics, in which policy-making sometimes appears to take place live on television before our very eyes, is entirely to the benefit of the nation. He considers that the medium is in danger of overtaking the message and that things have got to the point where one sometimes wonders whether more time is not spent discussing policy on the air than in deliberating on it in private.[18]

The excessive workload of ministers, their frequent rotation and the inordinate attention given to the media are all seen as problems which limit the capacity to make good policy. But they are, in a sense, incidental to the policy-making process itself. Some critics believe that

that process has been eroded over time and by new importations.

It is the perception of some, but by no means all, commentators that the Cabinet's role in policy-making has significantly diminished, that its role in decision-taking is now largely formal and that it is unsuited to strategic discussion. Ferdinand Mount, head of the Prime Minister's Policy Unit in 1982–3, writes that

> the Cabinet did not feel itself equipped to discuss difficult, long-term policy options; the fear of political embarrassment was too overwhelming to run the risk of being seen to examine such bleeding raw material. Implicitly, while continuing jealously to think of itself as the supreme executive body, Cabinet recognises that it is equipped only to approve dishes that are at least three-quarters cooked.

Originating a phrase that was later to be repeated by Peter Mandelson,[19] Mount says of the Cabinet, 'It is not itself the cook, and the Cabinet room is not the kitchen.'[20] The actual location of the kitchen is a matter to which I shall return.

It is commonly recognized that many policy decisions are, and have long been, taken by Cabinet Committees rather than Cabinet but some writers believe that the status of these bodies has also been diminished and that many significant decisions are now taken in small, *ad hoc* groups of ministers or simply by the Prime Minister in consultation with one or two ministers who have a major interest. These, and other developments, are much discussed in the academic literature on the 'presidentializing' of the British system of government. The contention is that the British Prime Minister increasingly resembles the President of the United States in his or her ability to take policy decisions and drive the government machine, free, or relatively free, of the constraints of collective ministerial responsibility and other constitutional conventions. This thesis draws heavily on comments made by ministers such as Lord Howe, Lord Lawson and Mr Heseltine who resigned from Mrs Thatcher's administration and suggested that collective government had broken down and that the Prime Minister was increasingly relying on unorthodox advisers rather than ministerial colleagues and other conventional sources of policy advice.

Recognizing that the controversy about the sources of advice on which a Prime Minister should properly draw is of long standing, one writer argues that 'the presidentialization of the advisory system that had been continuous, if spasmodic, since 1964, was considerably advanced by Mrs Thatcher's long period in office'. By the 1990s the Cabinet was seen as comparable to its American counterpart in being just one of many advisory bodies orbiting the Prime Minister; its members had become 'front men' who were expected to sell the Prime Minister's policies publicly, the Prime Minister being apparently free to exploit tensions between the Cabinet, advised by Whitehall, and the various alternative advisers on his or her personal staff.[21] Other commentators express concern about the growth in influence of external or political advisers more generally. First used as parallel sources of political input in the 1960s, these advisers later, by this account, became competing ones and today are starting to direct policy, with civil servants, the classical source of advice, becoming 'prisoners rather than the gaolers of power . . . Whether this represents a triumph for democracy is another question.'[22]

The current role of civil servants in providing policy advice has attracted a good deal of comment. The balance of power is thought to have shifted from civil servants to ministers over the years. Ministers are held to treat civil servants now as implementers of their policies rather than as partners; insofar as they consult they fail to reflect the outcome in their policy-making. Party strategists and public relations advisers have, it is believed, become more important than the traditional civil service in devising policies to win elections and, therefore, in policy-making.[23] Whereas handling the political process was once the core competence *par excellence* of the mandarin class this has become the function of a network of interests: 'The literature on policy disasters demonstrates a decline in the commitment, on the part of civil servants, to present evidence-based analysis to ministers, perhaps the inevitable result of working for eighteen years for governments who believed they already knew the answers.'[24] The civil service attracts some blame for these developments, being criticized for the poor quality of its advice, for lack of vision and for failure to consult more than a narrow range of interests.

Several commentators believe that the emphasis in the last decade on the managerial as opposed to the advisory function of the civil service has had a deleterious impact on the policy-making process. One of the explanations offered for the policy 'disasters' described earlier is that the de-emphasis on policy work and the cult of manage-rialism have focused senior officials' attention on administrative reorganization and pushed policy advice work down the hierarchy.[25] A pamphlet produced in early 1997, based on discussion between the Labour Opposition front bench and former civil servants, and conceived as advice for an incoming Labour govern-ment, was blunt on the point:

> The management reforms in the civil service have resulted in a substantial de-layering and an over-emphasis on man-agement at the expense of policy development. Former Permanent Secretaries expressed serious anxiety that the policy-making capacity of the civil service had been undermined to such an extent that a new government with a different mind set and an appetite for fresh thinking would simply find that there was not sufficient capacity in some departments to develop the policies it wanted.[26]

The practice of 'new public management' has become, in the view of Peter Hennessy, one of the co-authors of the pamphlet, 'a mixture of comfort blanket and displacement activity for those who really have very little idea of what to do on the policy front'. In a lecture in Canada, from which this quotation is taken, Hennessy argued that because of the decline in respect for public service, which he attrib-utes to various causes, there is 'a tendency to lose sight of the intense and constant importance of policy analysis and policy advice produced in-house'. 'We live', he continued, 'in an era when the Armani-clad minds in the penumbra of fad- and fashion-prone private think-tanks can be preferred (especially if their advice comes gift-wrapped and suitably politically tinted) to that more sober, sometimes inconvenient fare served up by the tweed-clad minds in the career bureaucracy.' But, he insisted, 'the key ethic of the public service – fearless advice resting on top-class analysis, itself fashioned by evidence and reason – is not a marginal good, an optional extra. It is *the* crucial element in advanced and rational governance.'[27] Andrew Marr is similarly concerned about the implications for the ethic of public service of new developments such as the introduction of more people from the private sector into Whitehall and the creation of agencies. He believes that the success of the 1854 Northcote-Trevelyan report in producing 'a clean, clear area for public administration was a great and lasting achievement' and adds:

> One would have thought that any tampering with it, however necessary, would have produced a serious debate first and a cautious response afterwards. But no: all we had was a sudden coup followed by bland assertions that nothing had changed. Civil servants need a new kind of contract, and a new kind of training, if the essence of Northcote-Trevelyan is to be saved.[28]

The picture that emerges from this account, which is admittedly episodic and partial, is one of a distinct lack of confidence in the current policy-making process in Britain. There is considerable doubt as to whether policy-making is accorded sufficiently high priority by government and whether the process and those who operate it have the capacity (some might add the inclination) to produce well-thought-out and consistent policy. I have deliberately allowed this summary of external views to stand by itself rather than interlarding it with observations of my own because, even if it is believed by those who have worked, and still work, in government, to be unfounded or inaccurate (though I doubt if many would regard it as wholly incorrect), it is of some importance that the public perception of the process and its problems receives attention. Nobody concerned with good government can feel comfortable with a situation where there is such widespread doubt about the ability to make good policy.

That said, before I turn to foreign policy-making, I should state that I do not regard all the criticisms I have described as well based. Indeed, I believe that, taken together, they give far too gloomy a picture of the state of policy-making in Britain. The assertion that Britain, measured against other comparable European democracies, and perhaps liberal democracies in general, is unusually prone to make large-scale policy mistakes does not seem to me to have been demonstrated in the academic literature. It would need a good deal of comparative research to establish the charge. It is also clear to me that concern about the quality of policy-making extends well beyond Britain and I shall deal with that point rather more fully later on. But it is worth noting here that when, in late 1996, senior civil servants from the OECD countries met to consider the matter, it was reported afterwards that *all* the governments represented were worried about policy capacity. Then, too, a rounded judgement on the quality of policy decisions in Britain must surely embrace the successes as well as the failures. Many who remember the condition of Britain in the late 1970s will be inclined to think that the period since then has on the whole been one of policy success, in macro-economic policy, in industrial restructuring, in the recovery of British prestige abroad and much else. Nor am I altogether persuaded that the disparate collection of alleged policy failures cited at the beginning of this chapter – from the ERM episode to the case of the London Ambulance Service – can be ascribed to similar causes (and indeed the need for further research on the causes is admitted by at least some of the critics). But I do not doubt that many of the explanations advanced by outside observers are valid. The excessive workload of ministers, their frequent rotation, the crowding-out of other functions by the time spent on presentation, all ring true.

The proposition that the policy-making process has been eroded by a decline in collective government and the so-called 'presidentializing' of the Prime Ministership seems somewhat more doubtful. I do not detect a significant trend. The relationship between Prime Ministers and their ministerial colleagues seems to me to have fluctuated over the years, depending on personalities, the political strength of the party in power, the personal standing of the Prime Minister and so on. In my view this thesis places too much weight on a particular period of eleven years when, unusually, one Prime Minister held the reins. The assertion that the presidentialization phenomenon is demonstrated by the range of personal and unofficial advisers on whom Prime Ministers now draw, in preference to the conventional sources of advice, seems to me exaggerated. In my experience external advisers, in particular the category known as political advisers, have been successfully integrated into the system of government within well-understood parameters and both the politicians they advise and the departments in which they sit have generally benefited. The role of particular named advisers is often greatly exaggerated, perhaps because of the appetite for personalization of politics and government which the media stimulates and attempts to satisfy. In my time as Private Secretary to the Prime Minister (1981–4) I often read with interest, and I am afraid some amusement, accounts of how influential with Mrs Thatcher particular advisers both within and outside No. 10 Downing Street were thought to be. As a matter of fact I often knew otherwise.

The functioning of the Cabinet and Cabinet Committees in policy formulation has been the subject of many studies. It is not, I think, contested by anyone that the role of Cabinet in this area has greatly diminished over the years. Examination of the archives related to the first two or three governments after the Second World

War shows the Cabinet deeply involved in often lengthy discussion of major policy issues on the basis of weighty papers, a description which no one would recognize as true of Cabinet in more recent times. As to the importance of Cabinet Committees in policy decisions, general statements can be misleading. Some play a bigger role than others. The pattern constantly shifts. Case studies are more valuable than generalizations. But since Cabinet archives in general remain closed for thirty years it is virtually impossible for scholars to produce case studies that have much relevance to contemporary government.

It will be clear from the Preface that I agree with the observation that the new emphasis in the last decade or so on the management functions of civil servants has eroded their role in advising on policy. As Permanent Under-Secretary at the Foreign Office I struggled to fulfil my responsibility, described in the Department's Annual Reports to Parliament, 'for providing advice on all aspects of foreign policy to the Foreign Secretary' precisely because my second declared responsibility 'for the management of the FCO . . . and the Diplomatic Service' assumed such large dimensions. Constant reviews of management and expenditure required by the centre as well as new management initiatives which Permanent Under-Secretaries were expected personally to supervise, coupled with the day-to-day tasks of managing a major department of state and a world-wide diplomatic service, ate into the day to the extent that well over fifty per cent of my time was spent on management issues. I was not alone. Indeed, I may have been more fortunate than some, for at least two colleagues in other major departments told me that in their case senior staff had become so preoccupied with management that they had virtually withdrawn from the function of providing policy advice, that task having been delegated to junior staff. The management revolution has brought great benefits to departmental administration but some re-allocation of priorities so that civil servants can carry out their primary function of advising ministers on policy is, in my view, well overdue. Indeed, there is much more to be said about the observation of outsiders that the classic relationship between ministers and civil servants has been eroded and, in the interest of good government, should, with modifications, be restored. But I shall reserve comment on that to a later discussion of current problems in the policy-making process and possible solutions.

The range of domestic policy is vast. A satisfactory account of how well it is made, of the successes and failures, would be a major study in itself and one that I am not sufficiently well-qualified by experience to carry out. The rest of this book deals with an area with which I am more familiar. But it is clear enough that concern about policy-making extends across the range of government activity. Some of the discussion about the making of foreign policy will clearly be relevant to the domestic area. Some may be less so. But as the dividing line between foreign and domestic policy becomes increasingly blurred (a theme discussed in Chapter 5) it is likely that most lessons from one area will apply to the other.

2

FLOATING DOWNSTREAM?

'English policy', said Lord Salisbury, 'is to float lazily downstream occasionally putting out a diplomatic boat-hook to avoid collisions.'[1] The image hints at most of the flaws which, for many students of Britain's international activity, explain the historical weaknesses of foreign policy-making: an inflated notion of Britain's capacity and influence, a failure to adjust to reality, an overweening trust in pragmatism and reaction to events as they occur, an inability to plan ahead and set clear objectives, and a disinclination to define publicly an international role for Britain and persuade public opinion of its merits. In this chapter I examine these themes before, in the next, considering the various attempts by British governments to review British foreign policy, and, in subsequent chapters, setting out my own views on the way the process works today, on the nature of foreign policy at the close of the millennium, on desirable improvements to the process, on lessons that can be drawn from the practice of another country (Australia), and, finally, on possible concepts of a British role in the world. I do not try to describe the substance of British foreign policy over the years, for that is beyond the scope of this book. Although it is easy to come by critical studies of episodes regarded as failures of foreign policy-making, for example the Suez intervention of 1956, the events leading to the Argentinian invasion of the Falklands in 1982 or the more recent case of Bosnia, the general burden of external criticism is directed more at the sins implied by Lord Salisbury's boating image than at specific cases of failure, though Britain's inability to establish a satisfactory relationship with continental Europe is a recurring theme which will necessarily form part of the discussion.

The starting point for many writers is Britain's reduced strength after the Second World War and its subsequent decline. If the country had been clear about its international role before 1939 it found it harder to produce that clarity thereafter. Winston Churchill famously advanced the concept of the Three Circles – the United States, Europe and the Commonwealth – the key areas where he believed Britain could sustain special relationships and exercise important influence. Some observers argue that in the circumstances this was a reasonable guiding strategy since these were precisely the areas where British interests and scope for influence were greatest. Objectively, Britain *did* retain more widely ranging

responsibilities and interests than other European states
and had more capacity to concern itself with global order
than continental Europe, which, more devastated by the
war, had to focus its energies on national reconstruction
and security.[2] But for some the Churchillian concept
already contained the seeds of that failure to adapt to
reality which was to be such a marked feature of British
policy in the following decades. One author writes even
more scathingly that the concept, 'represented as the
essence of wisdom, could equally well be described as a
biblical text for the justification of strategic indecision'.[3]
Yet it was at least an attempt to define the country's overseas purpose. Many writers have sought in vain ever since
for an adequate alternative description of the British role
by policy-makers. While British standing in the world
progressively declined and that world became increasingly interdependent, Britain pursued its ambition to
remain a global power and an autonomous actor. As
Empire faded into Commonwealth and the relationship
with the United States became less special, British
governments seemed unable to formulate a new grand
strategy.

Partly because the loss of national autonomy was disguised
and diffused by the partnership with the United States in
an English-speaking world; partly because free trade and
openness to refugees have become parts of the British
national myth; partly because the war-time experience
reinforced the sense of national solidarity and revalidated
the symbols of national identity for Britain, successive

governments have adjusted to increasing interdependence and decreasing British standing in the world without thinking it necessary to redefine national goals or to launch an organised debate about history and identity.[4]

Seventeen years after the end of the war the former US Secretary of State, Dean Acheson, delivered a speech to an American audience, one paragraph of which caused consternation in London at the time. Perhaps because it has seemed close to the uncomfortable truth for Britons then and since, it has proved as memorable as Churchill's 'Three Circles' concept, or at least its first sentence has:

> Great Britain has lost an Empire and has not yet found a role. The attempt to play a separate power role – that is, a role apart from Europe, a role based on a 'special relationship' with the US, a role based on being the head of a 'Commonwealth' which has no political structure, unity, or strength, and enjoys a fragile and precarious economic relationship by means of the Sterling area and preferences in the British market – this role is about to be played out. Great Britain, attempting to work alone and to be a broker between the United States and Russia, has seemed to conduct policy as weak as its military power.[5]

Nearly forty years later Britain still has a number of overseas territories for which it is responsible and a relationship of special character with the United States, and the Commonwealth survives. But the heart of

Acheson's comment, that Britain had ideas above its economic and military station, is regarded by most historians as accurate enough.

In trying to explain the persistent pursuit of illusion rather than reality much weight is attached to the attitudes and assumptions of those who made policy. Sir Oliver Franks said in 1954, 'It is part of the habit and furniture of our minds' that Britain should continue as a great power.[6] Britain, for the post-war generation of policy-makers, had always had a special place in ordering the affairs of the world. The idea that it might abandon a global perspective probably did not occur. This would have seemed quite at odds with the global spread of British interests and responsibilities and what was expected of British governments, by both popular opinion and the world community. 'Inflated ideas of Britain's role, part overestimate, part wishful thinking by leaders and led alike, persisted for many years.'[7] The Prime Minister, Harold Wilson, said in 1965 that we were a world power and a world influence or we were nothing. Britain's frontiers, he also proclaimed, rested on the Himalayas.

Political strategy, the argument continues, designed to preserve influence in all three of Churchill's circles, took insufficient account of the nation's depleted resources. Economic strategy envisaged a role in the world which the domestic economy was not strong enough to support and sought, in particular, to restore sterling to something approaching the 'top currency' reserve role that it had enjoyed at the height of Empire. The liquidation of military bases east of Suez in 1972 signalled a formal retreat from the concept of a global defence role. But continuing high expenditure on defence as a proportion of GDP suggests to some historians that in that field, too, the post-imperial Great Power 'syndrome' persisted.[8] The policy-makers, it is argued, continued to construe policy essentially in power terms, force being considered to play a vital role in inter-state relations, and paid a great deal of attention to US–Soviet confrontation. In order to arrest the decline in British power, the 'special relationship' with the United States was nurtured, the independent nuclear deterrent was maintained and high priority was given to sustaining military capability in general to enable Britain to exert influence in excess of its real capacity to project power. The country was failing to recognize the growing interdependence of the states of the world, the reduced scope for independence and autonomous decision-making. Even when, as the years progressed, policy was necessarily adjusted to the requirements of interdependence, the power-projection approach was retained, leading to inconsistency and ambiguity in policy.[9]

The gloomy picture of decline continues, at least into the late 1970s, still accompanied by a failure to elucidate a clear overseas role for the country and, by some accounts, still hampered by over-extended international activity. The picture changes to some extent during Mrs Thatcher's period in office when Britain is regarded as having played a more forceful and successful role on the world stage. But then another theme emerges in the commentaries – a failure to adjust to the end of the Cold

War and to redefine Britain's objectives in the fundamentally changed world situation brought about by the end
of superpower confrontation and the break-up of the
Soviet Union. What was required in the early 1990s was
'a thorough reconsideration of the relationship between
the British state and its neighbours, allies and rivals – and
of the instruments and expenditure the British state
should supply'.[10] Both the world and the nature of
foreign policy had changed radically but observers could
not detect a commensurate change in the British
approach. The British government would either just be
dragged along in the wake of these changes or it would
'have to redefine its role and rationale . . . in language
which can persuade its audience, both within Britain and
outside, that it still has a distinctive and valuable contribution to make'.[11]

Unsurprisingly, a strong and consistent criticism in discussion of British foreign policy since 1945 relates to the
failure to define and achieve a satisfactory relationship
between Britain and the European mainland. The literature is large but the general story is well-known so I
confine myself to describing the main strands of criticism
in so far as they illuminate the policy-making process.
Much of the uncertainty about Britain's proper role in
the world is attributed to a failure of assessment – a
failure to appreciate not just the constraints imposed by
the country's declining economic strength but also the
growing unreality of the Churchillian concept of the
Three Circles as trade with the Empire/Commonwealth
decreased and trade with Europe grew; failure, also, to

appreciate the developing reality of the drive towards unity on the European mainland, the latter being underestimated throughout the whole period from the 1950s to the present day. A subsidiary theme is the failure to recognize the persistent strength of the Franco-German axis at the centre of European development.

The answer to the problem of national uncertainty about the direction and content of foreign policy was, it is suggested, available long ago for those who cared to see it. In a paper submitted to an all-day Cabinet discussion on Europe at Chequers in October 1966, Sir Con O'Neill, head of the UK Delegation to the European Communities, wrote:

> For the last twenty years this country has been adrift. On the whole, it has been a period of decline in our international standing and power. This has helped to produce a national mood of frustration and uncertainty. We do not know where we are going and have begun to lose confidence in ourselves. Perhaps the point has now been reached when the acceptance of a new goal and a new commitment could give the country as a whole a focus around which to crystallize its hopes and energies. Entry into Europe might provide the stimulus and target we require.[12]

But even after Britain had entered the European Community the uncertainty persisted. Unable to commit itself with the same enthusiasm as its European partners to the further development of the Community and intent on preserving its autonomy of action in many fields, Britain proved a difficult partner, still placing too much reliance on its relationship with the United States and still being unwilling to sacrifice its global perspective sufficiently to concentrate its resources and ambitions on Europe.

The policy-makers, say the outside critics, signally failed to explain the purposes and merits of membership to British public opinion.

> The political and administrative élite has never really attempted to create a domestic consensus to underpin Britain's European commitment. To the extent that membership was 'sold' to the British public during the 1970s, the measurable costs of entry were under-emphasised and set against the unexplained and immeasurable political benefits.[13]

There was no lack of official statements and there was plenty of public debate. But those who advocated policy were less than frank with their audience.

> There were ways and ways of presenting [the argument] to the public, and the most open way was not always selected. That was especially true of the deepest, most inchoate question: what membership of 'Europe' truly meant for national sovereignty. This was the issue which, if it proved to have been falsely handled, lay in wait to invalidate at its innermost core the nation's 'full-hearted consent'.[14]

For another writer the most remarkable aspect of the long story of Britain's relationship with the European

Community was that at no point was there 'a clear public explanation of the alternative, no wider debate in which the government attempted to educate public opinion and the opposition to emphasize the political consequences, not only of entry, but also of staying out'.[15] For these and other reasons British membership failed to provide the focus which Sir Con O'Neill had advocated and around which the nation's hopes and energies could crystallize. As the saga continued there was another consequence for foreign policy-makers: the debate about 'Europe' became so controversial and politically charged that discussion of other issues in Britain's international relations was to a large extent side-lined. This made the task of defining and winning support for an overall foreign policy a good deal more difficult.

Yet neither with respect to Britain's world role in general nor to its European role in particular is the assessment of observers so uniformly critical as the above summaries suggest. Some are wary of hindsight. It is easy enough to say after the event that Britain should have adjusted its aspirations more quickly in relation to its declining strength. But at any given time the likely future rate of decline was hard to predict and the actual rate was probably quicker than most would have expected. The record and pace of disengagement from imperial commitments were by no means generally discreditable given the need to prepare colonies for independence and not just scuttle.[16] The reduction of the British role to a purely European one was not a realistic policy option during the long period of the Cold War when the containment of

Communism and Soviet ambition was a clear national interest and Britain had the capacity to make a contribution to that end. British influence and experience in Asia, the Middle East and Africa were important Western assets in the global struggle with the Soviet Union.

The debate about decline is regarded by some as exaggerated and confused. It is misleading to compare the *image* of British power in 1945 with the *reality* in the late twentieth century. Britain has, according to some indicators, grown steadily stronger since 1945 with standards of living improving exponentially. Certainly there has been *relative* decline, that is in relation to some other comparable states, but 'given that, after a hundred years of "decline", Britain is still one of the wealthiest and most powerful states in the world, perhaps those who have been managing its decline should be congratulated for slowing it down so effectively'.[17] Finally, much of the talk of decline dates from the period before the 1980s, but the attention that many other countries paid thereafter to successful reform and economic progress in Britain does not sit comfortably with the notion of irresistible decline.

I also question whether the charge that successive British leaders failed to follow the obvious course of concentrating on the European option is historically sensitive. Some argue that a firm decision to make Europe the top priority of foreign policy should have been taken many years ago. My own view is different. At most given moments in the story the option was probably never very clear-cut. On any objective assessment significant British interests were spread around the globe and could not be lightly abandoned. The psychological impact on the British people of retreat from Empire and the visibly declining power of their country may even now not have run its course. For most EC member states, fundamental political and/or economic factors dictated the need to belong to the European organization. In Britain's case the need was not so clearly compelling. These were realities that it is easy to underestimate in the late 1990s.

But this account of the perceived weaknesses in the policy-making process is not yet complete. There is an important strand of comment which focuses on attitudes and methods and points to a lack of vision, strategy or, simply, objectives, a preference for pragmatism and *ad hoc* reaction, an incapacity to plan and predict, a disinclination to embark on creative or preventive diplomacy, a failure to exploit assets and apportion expenditure rationally, and a reluctance to engage in serious public debate about foreign policy. Before examining the process as seen from the inside, it is worth looking at these themes.

For some critics, it is the lack of strategy or 'vision' which weakens British foreign policy, the absence of a single overarching concept or design, an 'Idea of Britain' which would inform more detailed objectives and the day-to-day thrust of diplomatic activity. The actions of the policy-makers over the years suggest that they have not been guided by any such strategy. Nor can the researchers find, at any rate in recent times, any public description which fits the bill. The absence of strategic thinking is held to have prevented clear and credible policies on individual issues, for example on Britain's role in Europe generally or on German reunification in particular.[18] As stated above, the need for a fresh and general definition of Britain's purpose abroad was particularly felt in the late 1980s and early 1990s when the collapse of the Soviet Union so radically changed the nature of the international environment. Then outsiders sought but could not find 'some formal statement of Britain's perceived and desired place in the world, an expression of a collective sense of self and the derivative objectives that Britain's foreign policy pursues'.[19] The problem is seen as infecting the whole process of foreign policy-making. A former Secretary of State for Defence said in 1987, 'No British Prime Minister since the 1960s has been sufficiently devoted to international strategy to think of defence policy within a broader vision of the international system and Britain's place in it.'[20] The foreign policy élite at large are regarded by some academic writers as averse to visionary thinking.[21] This is seen as partly a matter of inherited attitudes, to be dealt with below, partly a matter of system. The Whitehall culture of interdepartmental compromise and the practice whereby the formulation of policy advice begins at the lowest level are believed to inhibit a strategic approach.[22]

A former head of the Foreign Office planning staff draws attention to the Annual Report of the US administration to Congress in 1972, drafted by Henry Kissinger for Richard Nixon, which states: 'Without an understanding of the philosophical conception on which specific actions were based, the actions themselves can neither be adequately understood nor fairly judged. This account of a year of intense action, therefore, properly begins with a brief review of the intellectual foundations on which those actions rest.' No British Prime Minister or Foreign Secretary in the second half of the twentieth century, it is suggested, can readily be imagined as putting his name to such words.[23]

Grand strategy and visionary thinking apart, observers find it hard to detect more specific objectives, more precise goals. It is said that they have never been clearly defined, that, consequently, the need for hard choices has been avoided and that there is a bureaucratic inertia which militates against such choice. These flaws are regarded as being at least partly concealed by the competence and efficiency of the machine in dealing with immediate problems. The present government has recognized this issue. The 1999 White Paper on Modernizing Government contains commitments to ensure that policy-making is more strategic and that policy-makers will be forward-looking in developing policies that matter, rather than simply reacting to short-term pressures.[24]

Various writers suggest that decisions on expenditure in foreign policy (and government expenditure more generally) also exhibit a lack of clarity about objectives and an inability to make difficult choices. In earlier times when 'overstretch', the existence of too many international commitments, was the principal problem, and more recently when a main aim of government has been to reduce public expenditure, they see a failure to decide rationally how much effort to devote to various components of overseas policy – to diplomacy, the armed forces and foreign aid – and to decide which international issues are worth taxpayers' money and which are not. More widely, there is the question of what proportion of overall government expenditure should be devoted to foreign policy, where again the critics see an absence of conscious choice. The end of the Cold War is particularly identified as a time when the opportunity to redistribute resources was missed. 'Many observers have argued that a broad and rational approach to British external relations would long ago have cut the defence budget and reallocated resources to some of the less tangible aspects of diplomatic relations.'[25]

The machine itself is seen by some as incapable of organizing a fundamental redistribution of resources between Whitehall departments. In the pamphlet prepared for an incoming Labour government in early 1997, already quoted, it is stated that 'There is widespread agreement that the way in which the total level of public borrowing is currently arrived at, and the processes which determine how it is then distributed between different departments, is flawed.' Commenting on the activities of EDX, the Cabinet Committee which under the previous administration had annually recommended budgetary allocations to Cabinet, the pamphlet states, 'Decision-making has not been based on clear political assessment of the relative value of competing claims, and the funding of some programmes rather than others has not followed any clear criteria. Indeed, there has been a drift back to the *ad hoc* horse-trading that went before.'[26]

What, then, according to the critics, are the root causes of the failure to define purposes, to make deliberate choices, to develop both rational and farsighted foreign policy? Much is attributed to the British character. George Orwell wrote that 'the English will never develop into a nation of philosophers. They will always prefer instinct to logic, and character to intelligence.'[27] Or, as Philip Ziegler has said, 'As a nation we do seem to be empiricist, extremely cautious about principles, strong on pragmatism, and we just *are* a sort of back-of-the-envelope-type race.'[28]

Some practitioners of foreign policy have made no bones about their pragmatic approach to their trade. Before the Second World War Lord Halifax said 'I distrust anyone who foresees consequences and advocates remedies to avert them.'[29] A later Foreign Secretary, Lord Carrington, states in his memoirs: 'I am a pragmatist. I have found all my life that the gulf between what is theoretically desirable and what is practically attainable is so wide that it is sensible to concentrate almost exclusively upon the latter.'[30] Sir Percy Cradock says of Lady Thatcher that she saw foreign policy 'not as a continuum . . . but rather as a series of disparate problems with obtainable solutions, or even as a zero sum game, which Britain had to win'.[31] From my own days as her Private Secretary I vividly recall that one of her most persistent questions was: 'What's the next thing?' Some piece of business had just been transacted, some decision taken, and the prime ministerial mind wanted to know what the next practical problem was which had to be settled. Not much reaching for an overall policy concept there. Officials were not immune from the *ad hoc* approach to policy-making. I do not know which Deputy Under-Secretary in the Foreign Office told one historian that 'Our skill is in *not* having a grand strategic concept'[32] but I recognize the style.

So the fault, if it be a fault, may lie partly in innate British characteristics but it also certainly owes a great deal to the very nature of foreign policy-making. For Lord Strang, Permanent Under-Secretary at the Foreign Office from 1949 to 1953, policy was often

> not a fully independent invention capable of guiding diplomatic action . . . it is a dominant or a prevailing trend, established only in part, if at all, by premeditated and predetermined intention, and revealing itself through the cumulative effect of a succession of individual acts of greater or lesser moment, each decided upon in the light of practical international possibilities as they manifested themselves at the relevant time and under the impulse of a traditional manner of behaviour characteristic of the government concerned.[33]

Much foreign policy, the commentators would agree, is bound to be reactive. Britain is only one of many actors on the stage. Many overseas events are unpredictable or have not been predicted. A quick British reaction to an international development is often essential. Or it is necessary to respond to some sudden movement of public opinion, increasingly produced by the pervasive media. One former practitioner goes so far as to say that the principle which governed the Foreign Office during his period of service (1947–80) was the 'conditioned reflex', whereby a stimulating impulse, whether a message from abroad, an input from domestic politics or occasionally a 'spurt of initiative' from a minister or official, evoked a response from the machine.[34] Moreover, as he and other practitioners would point out, the machinery is largely designed for, and closely geared to, the need for quick reaction. It is the diplomat who is most adept at responding intelligently, decisively and speedily to these impulses who secures the praise and is most likely to advance, not the long-term thinker, not the philosopher.

Skill in reaction is not, however, the same thing as pragmatism. The latter ought to mean a disposition to look at the facts realistically and to accept the unpleasant choice phlegmatically if it is dictated by the facts. But it is an attitude which can also lead to the avoidance of major choices and adherence to what one has. If you are the only boat on the river, or if the others are insignificant in terms of comparable power, floating lazily downstream may be an effective way of getting where you want to. But Britain has long ceased to be in that position. The essentially passive approach was probably apt so long as Britain's resources were adequate 'to cope with challenges to her position, security and welfare . . . but now that Britain's operational reserves have dwindled and the challenges multiplied it is a fair question whether it is not itself a considerable source of weakness'.[35]

If the British tradition is one of pragmatism and reactive policy-making and if that disposition is reinforced by the very nature of foreign policy, it is not surprising that weakness has been detected in the capacity of governments and officials to plan, in the formal sense, and to think ahead. Peter Hennessy has referred to a decline over thirty-five years in the capacity of British central government to think in depth about the long term.[36] Whether there has been so consistent a trend is debatable. Some writers discuss the weakness of planning in the 1950s, when both ministers and officials showed an aversion to such activity and a preference for practical administration, but record deliberate attempts in the 1960s to strengthen the planning apparatus and construct a more coherent foreign policy, only to note that in the 1980s 'there was almost no demand for long-term thinking on international issues within government'.[37] In that latter period, government seemed to regard long-range documents on policy issues as hostile to conviction politics. Although some such documents were rightly criticized as anodyne, they were at least systematic attempts to set out and deal with the main issues of the following ten years or more.[38]

The historians find few examples over the years of the Foreign Office itself planning for the future but note that the Ministry of Defence has done so fairly consistently, though they recognize that the latter was effectively compelled to do so because the lead time for the development and production of new weapons, and the need to obtain public support for the very considerable expenditure involved, required it to produce regularly a convincing analysis of the likely world environment a decade hence. Currently, the lack of adequate planning for the handling of new transnational issues on the international agenda, such as environmental threats, is also noted. If the practice of planning has been traditionally weak, it is not surprising that our capacity to think clearly about matters that are new to our experience is limited.[39]

Prediction is not the same as planning, but the two are closely connected. Failure to anticipate international developments is another charge laid by some at the Foreign Office door. Examples cited include a failure to see where events in the Middle East were leading before the Suez invasion of 1956, to expect and plan for the Unilateral Declaration of Independence in Rhodesia in 1965, to predict the Falklands invasion in 1982 and to foresee the break-up of the Soviet Union in the early 1990s and the subsequent disintegration of Yugoslavia. Much could be said about each of these episodes. Lord Owen records that the Foreign Office had for many years warned successive governments about the danger of Argentina taking over the Falklands.[40] Sir Percy Cradock has described the assessments by the Joint Intelligence Committee of the collapse of the Soviet Union and Yugoslavia.[41] I believe the record will one day show that the assessors were more successful in their forecasts than the critics suggest. I shall return to the problem of prediction but it is worth noting here that without a planning and predictive capacity the possibility of effective preventive diplomacy – intervening to prevent a situation which you judge will occur and will harm – tends to vanish.

There is one more strand of criticism to describe before this catalogue closes. It is argued that successive governments have long been reluctant to produce regular and comprehensive descriptions of British foreign policy that might inform public debate. This complaint may strike both the ministerial and the official practitioner as peculiarly odd given the amount of time and effort which are put into the preparation and delivery of speeches and statements on foreign policy for parliamentary and wider public purposes. But the criticism is more specific – that, unlike some foreign governments, our own does not compile and publish on a regular basis a single statement of the overall objectives of policy as distinct from, for example, White Papers on aspects of European policy or ministerial speeches on specific issues such as Bosnia. The matter has a long history. In June 1944, a senior Foreign Office official recommended that a two-year policy statement should be produced and updated every six months. 'That way', replied Sir Alexander Cadogan, the Permanent Under-Secretary, 'lies Bedlam.' In 1946, on becoming a junior minister at the Foreign Office, Christopher Mayhew asked to see a document, which he presumed existed, outlining foreign policy. He was told not only that no such document existed but also 'that it was really rather doubtful whether we had a foreign policy in that sense at all'.[42] Over the years, the idea of an annual White Paper on foreign policy recurred fairly frequently, but I do not think it was ever adopted (and it has certainly not been the practice in recent years). An anomaly is noted. Each year, the Ministry of Defence *does* produce an annual statement on the defence estimates. This has come to have increasing policy content so that it is now the nearest thing we have to an annual statement on foreign policy. But the Foreign Office produces no equivalent. 'Apparently it is not necessary to explain, regularly and in one place, what are the basic purposes of the . . . bundle of policy – much of it actually reactivity – that historians later regard as British foreign policy.'[43]

The works which I have consulted display less concern than I had expected about the 'secrecy' of foreign policy-making. It appears to be well understood that diplomatic activity cannot generally be conducted in the public domain. But the need for a well-articulated, overall statement of Britain's overseas purposes is clearly felt. I shall return to this issue later.

This chapter should conclude with some brief international comparisons. Are the perceived weaknesses in British foreign policy-making described above unique to Britain? In her survey of a number of the world's foreign ministries, Zara Steiner finds that they have several problems in common. The *ad hoc* and pragmatic nature of most decision-making has militated against the development of long-range or predictive planning. Policy-planning bodies have been established but have rarely fulfilled the hopes of their founders.

Comprehensive reviews of foreign policy have rarely found an appreciative readership within the system. Efforts in these directions have repeatedly been abandoned despite the knowledge of the importance of long-range forecasting.[44]

Comparisons with individual foreign countries are often of limited value because their system of foreign policy-making is frequently so different from that of Britain that no very clear lessons can be drawn. Those, such as France, whose foreign policy is very much the preserve of the head of state, and where there are less well-developed mechanisms for debating and contesting foreign policy goals, seem more easily to produce overarching visions of the country's international aims and purposes and, perhaps, greater consistency in policy over time. Whether their foreign policy is more successful as a result is another question. Germany, too, has demonstrated particular consistency in foreign policy goals, partly because the frequency of coalition governments dictates the need for inter-party consensus. Once achieved, the participants are reluctant to unravel it. In the view of one expert on Germany, it has had one of the most consistent foreign policies of any Western power, a blend of Adenauerian Westpolitik and Brandtian Ostpolitik, based on the principles of renunciation of force, reconciliation with former foes, the pursuit of national goals through multilateral institutions and negotiation, and the conflation of German and European interests. He considers that the country now needs to make clearer choices than in the past. But, he believes, it will choose not to choose.[45]

Canada's system of policy-making is broadly similar to that of the United Kingdom. In 1995 the Canadian government established a task force to consider the problem of policy-making. Its report began with the statement that 'There has for some time been a sense that all might not be right with the policy capacity of the Federal Government.' It noted some of the same problems inhibiting good policy-making which were described in the last chapter; emphasized that a sustained demand from the top for high-quality work was the essential condition for improvement; judged that the most notable weaknesses related to longer-term strategic and horizontal issues; and made a series of recommendations to strengthen policy capacity both within individual departments and across the system.[46]

The making of foreign policy in Canada has not escaped criticism. One scholar recently observed that the Federal Government's 1995 statement on 'Canada and the World' displayed no attempt to define priorities amid shrinking resources. Policy tended to focus on 'splashy agenda-setting' and 'announceability' rather than substance. Increased activism in 'declaratory' foreign policy had been accompanied by a slash-and-burn approach to the management of Canada's foreign policy instruments, with cuts in the defence, aid and foreign affairs budget, so that greater activism was combined with atrophy in capability. The Canadian International Development Agency, responsible for aid to the developing world, had reached the point where it had no substantial in-house policy development capability and relied on international organizations and non-governmental organizations for policy-development inputs. The major problems with Canada's foreign policy resulted from, among other things, its conceptual basis and the persisting ambiguity about where Canada fits in a post-Cold War structure of international politics.[47]

The least useful source of lessons for the British foreign policy-making system is the United States, not just because of its superpower status and all that goes with it, but because the process of making American foreign policy is so radically different. The centres of decision-making are multiple and diffuse (though all ultimately lead to the President); the tensions within the executive between the State Department, the Pentagon and the National Security Council are replicated only very weakly in other systems; and the in-fighting is much more public. But if these are constants in the system there is a large body of critical opinion which expresses deep concern about the decline in America's policy capacity. A 1984 study, subtitled *The Unmaking of American Foreign Policy*, argues that there has been 'a systematic breakdown when attempting to fashion a coherent and consistent approach to the world'. It asserts that the making of foreign policy has become far more partisan and ideological and that the White House has succumbed to 'the impulse to view the presidency as a public relations opportunity'. Any coherent sense of national interest has been lost: 'Serious nations do not redefine their national interests every few years, as we have been doing for most of the last two decades.' Wild swings in policy have become the norm.[48] Later critics point to the emergence, with President Carter, of the 'process president' who believes 'that if the process is good the product will be good', who places greater emphasis on methods, procedures and instruments for making policy than on the substance of policy.[49] The growing role of ethnic and other interest groups in influencing foreign policy is seen as making a defective system even less coherent. The United States 'has less of a foreign policy in a traditional sense of a great power than we have the stapling together of a series of goals put forth by domestic constituency groups. The result is that American foreign policy is incoherent. It is scarcely what one would expect from the leading world power.'[50] The recent dominance of commercial goals in American foreign policy attracts criticism as does, familiarly, the failure, especially in the wake of the break-up of the Soviet Union, to develop a new world view. One administration official is quoted as dismissing that notion as 'strato-crap and globaloney'.[51]

A balanced account of American foreign policy-making would, of course, need more detailed examination. But enough has been said about the United States and other countries to show that the concerns about foreign policy-making spread well beyond Britain. It is now time to move inside the system and establish whether, and if so how far, these concerns are justified, what the actual policy-making system is and how it can be improved.

3

NOT FOR WANT OF TRYING

Most foreign policy is not made as a result of fundamental reviews. It is constructed to deal with
specific situations or in reaction to specific events. But
since the majority of the criticisms in the previous chapter
are of a general nature and relate to a perceived lack of
strategy and objectives, it is worth looking at the various
studied attempts made by British governments since the
Second World War to review policy in general and the
assets and machinery available to pursue that policy. The
story begins at the end of the war but continues with gaps
to very recent times. When I left the Foreign Office in
1997 there was a feeling that, far from these matters not
having been addressed, we had been 'reviewed to death'.
A comprehensive account of all the general reviews that
have occurred would be far too bulky for this book.
Nevertheless, since successive governments *have*, in these

studies, attempted to address the questions of decline, overextension, changing world circumstances and objective-setting, a brief, selective summary, concentrating on those aspects which concern the process of making foreign policy, should throw a good deal of light on these issues. I cannot be entirely confident that I have uncovered all the fundamental reviews in the period. During the later years, for which the archives remain closed, there may be examples of which I was unaware or on which I cannot comment for the very reason that the archives *are* closed. But I do not think any omissions will prove to be numerous or very significant.

Even during the war the question of the desirable nature of the future Foreign Service was addressed. The so-called 'Eden Reforms' of 1943 amalgamated the Foreign Office and Diplomatic Service with the Commercial Diplomatic Service and the Consular Service to create a new Foreign Service. This was to be recruited and trained to deal with the whole range of international affairs, political and economic.[1] Immediately the war ended in Europe Anthony Eden, as Foreign Secretary, requested an account of the international situation. The result was a memorandum by Orme Sargent, a senior Foreign Office official, entitled 'Stocktaking after VE Day'.[2] Sargent addressed the two new post-war problems – the Soviet occupation of a large part of eastern Europe (and Soviet policy generally) and the economic rehabilitation of Europe. Contrary to the position in 1918, control of Europe was now largely in the hands of the United States and the Soviet Union. They were, he judged, unlikely to heed British interests unless we asserted ourselves. For they harboured the 'misconception' that Great Britain, numerically the weakest and geographically the smallest of the three great powers, was now a secondary power. They would be inclined to treat it as such. Having analysed Soviet and American intentions, the position of Germany and the situation in the Far East, Sargent concluded that policy should be based on the principle of co-operation between the three world powers. The British position should be strengthened by enrolling the Dominions, France and lesser Western European powers in our aims; we should not be afraid of having a policy independent of 'our two great partners'; our policy should be in keeping with fundamental British traditions, anti-totalitarian and liberal, taking risks and even living beyond our political means at times; and we should make every effort to grapple with the economic crisis in Europe. Eden agreed wholeheartedly and thought the paper and the annexes should be seen by the Prime Minister and perhaps the Cabinet. Policy here was being made largely between senior Foreign Office officials and the Foreign Secretary, no doubt exhibiting what in retrospect looks like an inflated perception of Britain's capacity but which, immediately after victory in Europe, can hardly have seemed so at the time.

Less than two years later things already looked very different. A 1947 memorandum by Gladwyn Jebb, another senior official, substantially revised Sargent's earlier assessment in the light of the development of the atomic bomb, the shift in the balance of military power

in Europe towards the Soviet Union, new evidence
of Soviet hostility towards the West, and the British
economic crisis 'which dominates and conditions
everything else'. In seventy-nine weighty paragraphs
Jebb analysed the British position throughout the world.
He concluded that Britain could now hardly follow a
policy independent of the United States, that it was
desirable to form a common diplomatic and economic
front with the countries of Western Europe and that we
should seek to achieve 'a proper balance between our
real strengths and our undertakings' but make no sacrifice until it was unavoidable. 'The British Lion is already
regarded as wounded; if he gives the impression of being
seriously ill the other animals are not likely to assist him
overmuch.'[3]

Cold dawn had arrived. The country's economic
problems were already uppermost in the minds of the
policy-makers. Various planning and other papers
appeared in the next few years, most attempting to define
British objectives in a rapidly evolving situation of
tension between the West and the Soviet Union and
envisaging a continuing 'world power' role for Britain
while recognizing the immense strain this was placing on
the British economy and in some cases considering how
far this could be relieved by shedding commitments. Two
papers by the Chiefs of Staff in 1950 and 1952, in the
aftermath of the formation of the Western Alliance and
the Soviet acquisition of the atomic bomb, formulated a
strategy to deal with the world-wide threat posed by the
Soviet Union.[4]

In June 1956 Sir Norman Brook, the Secretary to the Cabinet, minuted that the Prime Minister, Anthony Eden, proposed in the next few weeks to consider with the ministers immediately concerned what adjustments should be made in government policy in view of the change in methods, if not objectives, of the Soviet Union. The review would take account of Britain's economic and financial circumstances and would cover changes in domestic and overseas policy and adjustments to the defence programme.[5] The Policy Review Committee was to consist of the Prime Minister, Macmillan from the Treasury, Selwyn Lloyd from the Foreign Office, Monckton from the Ministry of Defence and Lord Salisbury (Lord President). A major memorandum on 'The Future of the United Kingdom in World Affairs' was prepared by officials of the Treasury, Foreign Office and Ministry of Defence.[6] It started from two premises. First, the hydrogen bomb had transformed the military situation and made full-scale war unlikely. Second, ever since the end of the war, Britain had tried to do too much and had rarely been free from the danger of economic crisis. Major decisions would be needed in all areas of policy, especially defence policy.

The main argument did not proceed from an assessment of British interests but, significantly, from the fact of Britain's strained economic situation. On the basis of present policies and commitments there was no prospect of being any more free of strain and crisis than we had been since 1945. A maximum internal and external effort was needed to reduce commitments. The prime

economic aim should be the maintenance of the international value of sterling, 'a matter of life or death to us
as a country'. So a detailed analysis should be made of
the additional resources needed to achieve adequate
investment at home, an adequate degree of flexibility in
industry and labour, and an adequate balance of payments surplus. Consumption should be reduced and
policies on external investment reviewed.

Overseas we should seek to reduce the present military
burden and develop non-military measures for the protection of our interests. Nuclear and thermo-nuclear
weapons brought military and political advantages more
cheaply than could be secured by other means. But the
size of Britain's nuclear and thermo-nuclear capacity
should be studied. A new NATO strategic concept
should be developed. Other detailed recommendations,
which covered many aspects of global policy, placed
much emphasis on reducing military commitments generally and maintaining British interests through the
development of non-military instruments.

The series of meetings planned by Eden to consider
this and other papers had begun when, in July 1956,
Egypt nationalized the Suez Canal and international
crisis followed. The policy review was effectively
suspended though one of its components, a general
review of defence policy, was completed by early 1957,
leading to further cuts in military commitments and in
the strength of the armed forces.[7] Several points are
worth making about this episode. First, this was a classic
exercise in policy formulation. The Prime Minister ini-

tiated a major review. Officials from the departments most closely concerned produced the jointly agreed paper described above (one of several prepared for the Committee) which took a broad view of the United Kingdom's position and future prospects. Deep ministerial involvement in discussion was planned. Doubtless the Review Committee would have reported to the full Cabinet but, not for the last time, this exercise in policy-making was negated by events. Although the formal context of the review was the change in methods, if not objectives, of the Soviet Union, the driving force was the United Kingdom's strained economic situation and its over-extension internationally. *En passant* it is interesting to note that it was proposed to compensate for reductions in military expenditure by devoting extra effort to other instruments of foreign policy, a theme which would often recur.

In November 1957, in the aftermath of the Suez crisis, another review was commissioned by the new Prime Minister, Harold Macmillan, and prepared by an official-level Cabinet Committee under the chairmanship of Sir Norman Brook. The Committee's report, entitled 'The Position of the United Kingdom in World Affairs', was submitted to the Prime Minister in June 1958.[8] It argued that although Britain could no longer operate from a position of material superiority it could still exercise a substantial influence, given its special position as a link between Europe, the Commonwealth and the United States. But it could not do so if it took refuge in the neutrality and comparative isolation of purely commercial powers like Sweden or Switzerland. Greater freedom of manoeuvre was needed in overseas policy. We now had to work largely through alliances and coalitions rather than by imposing our will. The basic policy aims were to prevent global war and defeat Russian and Chinese efforts to dominate, to maintain the free world's stability, to preserve the cohesion of the Commonwealth, to further our trading interests and to maintain the sterling area and the strength of sterling. Pursuit of these aims was hampered by a lack of resources but a fully effective policy would depend on the success of domestic economic policy. Additional expenditure of £5–6 million a year would be needed by the Foreign Office and the Commonwealth Relations Office to give them extra flexibility to counter the growing power of the Soviet Union, and extra loan finance would be needed for the colonies. But real flexibility in foreign policy would require more radical measures. Heavy cuts in the armed forces had already been decided on in Germany, Libya, Malaya and Hong Kong. Given these and other reductions in overseas commitments since the war, no further reductions could be made without significantly undermining our international position. It would be wrong to reduce further the priority given to our overseas commitments; no major reduction in defence spending could be expected in the near future; the right course was to consider cuts in domestic civil expenditure. At a meeting of Cabinet ministers on 7 July the Chancellor of the Exchequer agreed to consider sympathetically the proposed limited additional expenditure by the Foreign and

Commonwealth Offices and to discuss further the question of loan finance for colonial development.[9] He was also invited to consider cutting domestic civil expenditure in the longer term.

Despite the grand-sounding title of the paper which had been addressed this was more of a discussion about marginal expenditure than a fundamental review of foreign policy. But it is worth noting that the paper *did* lay down clear policy aims, even if taken together they have a somewhat unreal quality as tasks for a straitened Britain. It is worth noting, too, the continued close involvement of Cabinet ministers in foreign policy formulation for this is not a phenomenon which will continue throughout the period discussed in this chapter.

Less than a year later Macmillan launched another review. In June 1959, a group of senior officials and service chiefs were invited to Chequers to discuss with the Prime Minister an outline paper called 'Study of Future Policy'. It began with the question 'What developments can we foresee during the next ten years and what is likely to be the resulting situation in 1970?' It posed a series of other questions under this general heading and then invited a discussion of the desirable objectives for foreign policy, colonial policy and strategic policy during the next decade with an assessment of the consequences for public expenditure. Following work on these matters by officials during the rest of 1959 (Macmillan had always intended this paper to be available *after* the 1959 election), the Prime Minister circulated to Cabinet colleagues early the next year a paper called

'Future Policy Study, 1960–70'. He explained that its purpose was to try to forecast the state of the world in 1970 and the role that the United Kingdom would be able to play in it: 'I thought that, if they had this picture before them, ministers would be better able to formulate policies for the intervening years which would allow us to continue to play a significant part in world affairs.'[10]

The study, running to forty-seven pages, is a comprehensive piece of work from which I select only a few points. The first page recognizes that 'the European Economic Community is of immense potential importance. Their aggregate industrial power is probably greater than that of the USSR and if they continue to grow at their recent pace they will approach and perhaps reach the present United States level by 1970. If, therefore, the "Six" achieve a real measure of integration, a new world power will have come on the scene.' But after a lengthy analysis of the international prospects over the coming decade, of the country's resources and of the main objectives of overseas and strategic policy, the conclusions do not suggest that the time for a radical choice between Europe and the American relationship had arrived (according to a recent account Macmillan was determined to avoid such a choice, believing that Britain should belong to both camps and act as an intermediary between them; he had put Sir Norman Brook in charge of the exercise to ensure that the report reflected his thinking[11]). Instead, the report argued that we should work increasingly with and through our friends and allies. The core of policy should be the Atlantic alliance.

The main task should be to maintain and make more intimate the association between North America, the United Kingdom and continental Europe. We should do all we could to strengthen the Commonwealth. We should not expect to reduce the 8.5 per cent of GNP devoted to defence, aid and other overseas activities. The main problem was 'to keep the balance right between the competing claims, domestic and external, on the national resources and, within the resources applied to the support of external policy, between the claims for defence, for economic aid and for other overseas expenditure'.

Although Cabinet meetings were planned for late March 1960 to begin discussion of the study I have not been able to trace any record of Cabinet discussion (it is possible that Macmillan, as in the case of another study devoted to domestic matters, convened an unofficial meeting at Chequers which has not found its way into the records). Nevertheless, the study is of interest to the policy-making process. Once again, a major review had been launched by the Prime Minister. He had directly enlisted the participation of a group of Whitehall's most senior officials at the outset, explaining that he did not envisage other ministerial involvement at this stage of the policy review. The status accorded to officials in major foreign policy-making at this time is worth noting for it would tend to diminish later. The distinctive substantive feature of the review was that a considered attempt was made to predict the most likely evolution of the world situation a decade ahead. This was strategic and long-term planning at the highest level, for Macmillan had clearly intended intensive Cabinet discussion at a later stage. The struggle to define clear aims for overseas policy continued but the problem of choice apparently remained intractable for the authors of this document.

Yet little more than a year later negotiations began for possible British membership of the EEC. In this connection another striking instance of long-term planning occurred. In August 1961 a Long-Term Policy Group was established 'to study the long-term problems which seem likely to arise within the European Economic Community, and the policies which HM Government should pursue within it on the assumption that the United Kingdom was a member of it'. 'Long-term' was interpreted to mean up to 1975 and the twenty-three reports prepared on a wide range of external economic and trade issues and some internal EEC issues genuinely embraced that perspective.[12]

In the thirteen years between 1964 and 1977 Britain's overseas representation was formally reviewed on no fewer than three occasions. The Plowden Report of 1964 resulted in the amalgamation of the Foreign Service, the Commonwealth Service and the Trade Service in a unified Diplomatic Service and was mainly concerned with questions related to the future organization, recruitment and training of that service.[13] The Plowden Committee shared Churchill's view 'that Britain should not be content to be relegated to a tame and minor role in the world' but recognized that what could no longer be ensured by power alone should be secured by other means, making the best use of diplomacy and persuasion.

Commercial work should be a first charge on resources. As regards the policy process, the Committee noted that foreign policy now had a greatly increased public content, emphasized that good management should not be regarded as in any way inferior to policy work and laid considerable emphasis on planning. It felt that in the past some policy problems had not been anticipated or prepared for sufficiently and that some of the international issues in which Britain had been involved in the past two decades could have been better handled if their implications had been explored more fully in advance. Planning staff should be sufficiently free from current work to be able to germinate and develop ideas, without being so remote from current work that their thinking became too academic. Policy planning papers should be studied by senior officers with a firm responsibility for taking effective action and there must be a means of bringing these studies and recommendations to the attention of ministers: 'The . . . kind of policy planning . . . we think more useful . . . attempts to foresee the choices with which Britain is likely to be faced at some stage in the future and to consider how we can best use the intervening time to place ourselves in the best position to make a final choice when we have to.' We shall see later how far Plowden's injunctions on planning have been met in the policy-making process today.

Next, a somewhat mysterious affair. An article in *The Times* on 23 November 1967 stated that in the second half of 1966 a draft report examining the whole foundation of the government's economic and foreign policy was prepared but that when this came to the attention of the Prime Minister (Wilson) all copies except one were destroyed on his personal instruction. I have not been able to trace the surviving document, if it exists. Perhaps this was another review which came to nothing.

Four years after the Plowden Report the government appointed another committee to review Britain's overseas representation, this time consisting of a businessman (Sir Val Duncan, as chairman), a retired senior diplomat (Sir Frank Roberts) and a prominent journalist (Andrew Shonfield). In the light of the 1968 decision to withdraw military forces from east of Suez and the balance of payments situation, and the changing role which these implied for Britain, it was asked to review urgently the function and scale of the 'representational effort', to make recommendations in particular on the furtherance of British commercial and economic interests overseas, to bear in mind the current need for the strictest economy and the consequent desirability of providing British overseas representation at lesser cost, and to report within six months 'in order that the benefit of any savings may accrue as rapidly as possible'.

The Committee's report took the view that Britain had become a 'major power of the second order'.[14] It suggested that there was general agreement on certain major objectives of British external policy, the first three being improvement of the balance of payments, maintenance of the North American alliance and the promotion of integration in Western Europe. Its principal recommendations were based on a concept of the division of the world into two parts. The first was to be the 'Area of Concentration of British diplomacy', broadly speaking about a dozen or so countries in Western Europe together with North America and, perhaps, Japan and Australia. The distinctive feature of these countries was that Britain was likely to become increasingly involved with them 'to the point where none of us will be able to conduct our domestic policies without constant reference to each other'. The second was defined as 'the Rest of the World or Outer Area' where, though countries differed, 'none of them is likely to impinge on the day-to-day conduct of British Government business' in quite the way the countries of the first group were expected to do. The argument of the full report is more sophisticated than some later summaries have suggested, but having erected these two categories of countries (whose membership differed somewhat in different sections of the report) the Committee advocated comprehensive diplomatic missions in the Area of Concentration and 'selective missions', normally of only three UK-based officers, in the Outer Area. For export promotion purposes, on which the Committee laid great emphasis and made detailed recommendations, the world was divided somewhat differently. It was believed that savings of at least five per cent and perhaps as much as ten per cent of overseas expenditure could be achieved by the mid-1970s.

This was clearly an almost entirely cost-driven review, starting from the need to cut expenditure, not from an analysis of British interests. Again, some light is thrown on the policy-making process. In the closest that this kind of committee is likely to come to complaining, it stated that it was not possible to secure improved cost-effectiveness in the conduct of foreign policy by clarifying objectives and determining the scale of resources to be allocated to achieving them 'if there were ambiguities at the very centre of our policy decisions' (this was primarily a reference to the apparent intention to maintain a general military capability based in Europe which could be deployed overseas as circumstances demanded). Thus the Committee had been asked to review overseas representation without being given a sufficiently clear explanation of foreign policy objectives to allow it to do so properly. It also emphasized that in conducting international relations the government was reliant on the policy advice of its overseas representatives, a point to which I shall return in Chapter 6. The Committee struggled with the problem of prediction, to ensure that their recommendations were apt for the conditions in which British foreign policy would be operating in the mid-1970s. But it was precisely here that the Committee was later seen to have erred most seriously. Four years after its report the oil-producing countries raised oil prices markedly, provoking an international crisis. Relations with those countries suddenly became the focus of acute attention, but they were in the Outer Area where, had the Duncan Committee had its way, British representation would have been pared to a minimum. The episode serves as a warning of the hazards of prediction but also as an indication of how difficult that necessary task actually is. In fact, the Duncan Report was shelved after the June 1970 election and its concept of a divided world was never implemented.

In 1977 a third review of overseas representation was attempted, this time over fifteen months instead of a mere six, and was conducted by Sir Kenneth Berrill, head of the Central Policy Review Staff in the Cabinet Office, and six members of that unit. Its task was 'to review the nature and extent of our overseas interests and requirements and . . . to make recommendations on the most suitable, effective and economic means of representing and promoting those interests, both at home and overseas'. The report was much more wide-ranging and radical than its predecessors, covering not just the Foreign Office but all Whitehall departments and parts of departments responsible for making and carrying out overseas policies.[15] Its main purpose was not, according to the reviewers, to make economies.

Britain's status was seen as having steadily declined over twenty-five years. In the opinion of the reviewers, the overseas policies of governments had repeatedly failed to take sufficient account of this fact. Britain was now on a par with the three other medium-sized countries in the European Community. It would almost certainly take more than a decade for it to recapture an appreciable amount of the ground lost since 1945. If it was to have influence in the world this would increasingly be the result of influencing the policies pursued by the nine EC member-states as a whole. The country's four main objectives should be to ensure its security, promote its economic and social well-being, honour certain commitments and obligations, and work for a peaceful and just world. British overseas interests remained basically unchanged. What was different was the country's ability to promote and protect them.

Standing the Duncan Report on its head, Berrill took the view that British diplomatic activities should be reduced in the non-Communist developed countries since government effort was less necessary here than elsewhere to advance British interests. Permanent membership of the United Nations Security Council was not an unmixed blessing since it required greater involvement in UN affairs than British interests warranted. It was not necessary to devote large resources to the pursuit of the Commonwealth ideal. Disengagement from inherited commitments, where honourable and practicable, should be the objective, not because they were irrelevant to British interests but because our power to influence the situations related to those commitments was severely limited. The reviewers did not accept the arguments of others that this attitude was too defeatist; that Britain's membership of the Commonwealth and the EEC and its intimate relationship with the United States gave it a unique position; that it had national qualities which enabled it to play a special role in solving world problems; that British interests would suffer unless it maintained a presence equivalent to that of other 'major powers of the second order'; and that military and economic decline indicated a need for a greater, not smaller, diplomatic effort.

As in the case of Duncan, Berrill found that there was a policy gap. He was able to benefit from recent policy reviews in the defence, aid and immigration fields but in other areas found no policy guidance. 'One important policy question', the report impishly states, 'is the role that ministers believe the UK should play in the world.' To fill this gap the Berrill team produced their own suggested policies, not based on an analysis of British interests, narrowly defined, but on an analysis of the country's broad overseas objectives as they saw them.

Berrill's specific recommendations need not detain us long because, as will be seen, the main thrust of the report was not accepted by the government. He envisaged fairly widespread closures of diplomatic posts, a reduction by one-third in the work of political analysis and in the deployment of defence staff overseas, a substantial reduction in functions and staff in non-Communist developed countries, either the abolition of the British Council or a radical reorganization and reduction of its activities, a reorganization of export promotion machinery and the establishment of a new unit in the Cabinet Office to co-ordinate work on Britain's bilateral relations with overseas countries. The report put forward, as one alternative, the notion of merging the Home Civil Service and the Diplomatic Service and constituting within the new service a Foreign Service group to carry out overseas policy functions.

The Berrill Report was controversial, in Parliament and outside. The government replied firmly in August 1978.[16] British interests extended around the world. The country had the assets to defend those interests and promote its objectives. We had 'a more than adequate springboard for an imaginative and effective foreign policy' and our resources were adequate to support the system of overseas representation which such a foreign policy entailed. Britain's objectives overseas were clear: to safeguard the country's security, to promote its prosperity, to uphold democratic values, to honour commitments and obligations, to work for a peaceful and just world, and to provide assistance to developing countries. Assessment of our interests could not be confined to economic or exporting considerations alone. The government was making a special effort to explain publicly the objectives of foreign policy and to win support for its aims from public opinion.

In response to the report's main recommendations, and implicitly or explicitly rejecting many of them, the government said that it had decided to increase specialized knowledge in our overseas representation, to build a closer working relationship between the Diplomatic Service and the Home Civil Service, to improve co-ordination of overseas representation and the resources devoted to it, to have a Diplomatic Service fully responsive to government and British society, and to maintain a widespread and cost-effective system of residential representation overseas. But it would not integrate the Diplomatic and Home Services nor would it make any organizational change in export promotion arrangements. The overall conduct of overseas relations should remain the responsibility of the Foreign Secretary.

There was now a greater, not lesser, need for effective overseas representation precisely because our power as an individual nation was diminished. Some cuts would be made in the overseas effort (but they were mostly relatively minor in nature). Specifically on policy-making, the Foreign Office, in association with all relevant government departments, would in future produce country assessment papers providing basic policy guidelines for each country where Britain was represented, and from time to time departments would produce joint major policy papers on areas and issues of major importance, publishing these where possible.

Once again a major review had had limited impact though in this case the government had been stimulated to set out the objectives of foreign policy and define a concept, albeit very general in nature, of an overall British role in the world. There has been no review of this nature since, but in January 1995 a large group of ministers met at Chequers under the Prime Minister's chairmanship to consider Britain's overseas role. *The Times* commended the attempt, remarking that 'too often in the last four years policy has been formulated on the hoof in an atmosphere of barely suppressed anxiety'.[17] A biography of the then Foreign Secretary, Douglas Hurd, attributes the meeting to his strong feeling that, in the new post-Cold War environment, Britain needed to reassess its assets, identifying those areas where it could steadily increase its influence. But, by this account, although Hurd believed that he had secured the meeting's agreement to enhance the civilian side of the

overseas effort, the agreement did not come into opera-
tion because of subsequent objections by the Treasury.[18]

For completeness I should add that for many years now
the overseas effort has, in a sense, been reviewed almost
every year, first in the routine annual spending round by
which the allocation of government expenditure to
Whitehall departments was fixed (a different system has
obtained since the new Labour government came to
office in 1997) and then in larger exercises such as the
Fundamental Expenditure Review of 1995, the Senior
Management Review which followed and the
Comprehensive Spending Review of 1997/8. But this
kind of review was in effect cost-driven and rarely, if
ever, stemmed from a rational examination of Britain's
overseas interests and objectives, least of all in the final
decisions on expenditure taken at the end of each review.

The striking feature of the story in this chapter is how
little came of all the efforts devoted to reviewing policy.
Eden's 1956 attempt was blown off course by Suez.
Macmillan's 1958 review resulted only in marginal
expenditure decisions. His more ambitious effort in 1959
to review policy in a ten-year perspective was apparently
never discussed in Cabinet. The first review of overseas
representation (Plowden, 1964) was implemented but
was much more concerned with the internal organization of the Diplomatic Service than with foreign policy.
The second (Duncan, 1969) was shelved, perhaps fortu-
nately as events turned out. The third and most ambitious
(Berrill, 1977) foundered because its concept of Britain's
future role and its principal recommendations were

rejected by government, though some of its detailed recommendations were implemented. The latest (Chequers, 1995) came to nothing because of Treasury objections made after the event.

These reviews are only part of the picture. Much foreign policy was being made all the time elsewhere, quite independently of formal reviews, and had major outcomes, for example the 1968 decision to withdraw military forces from the area east of Suez and the decision to seek membership of the European Community. But it is apparent that none of the formal reviews discussed here produced a concept of Britain's overseas role which could both withstand the pressure of events and convince the government of the day of its inherent value and political credibility. The attempt to set clear objectives was constant but the formulation differed from review to review. Most of the exercises were cost-driven, either explicitly or because of the circumstances in which they were conducted. Rarely did the policy thinkers try to start from the bottom up, that is to define in some detail where British interests lay and then decide what the priorities were and how far they could be afforded. Despite the difficulty of defining national interests, to which I shall return, this method might have produced more convincing results.

From the point of view of process, it is striking, in contrast to today, how intimately Cabinet ministers were involved in planning and discussing future foreign policy, especially in the earlier part of the period. The role and status of officials in policy-making were similarly impressive.

But the difficulty of making choices and defining clear aims persisted. The Commonwealth declined as an object of attention over the years but more as a matter of fact than as a result of a policy decision. Even after Britain entered the European Community no attempt was made to 'choose' between Europe and North America in the sense of a decision to concentrate overseas policy resources on one at the expense of the other. The attempt to adjust to economic decline was continuous but the plateau was never reached where Britain could feel that it now had the measure of what it was trying to do overseas, and that the aims were clear and could be afforded.

Was the explanation, as some would say, incompetence or a failure to appreciate the true nature of Britain's circumstances and the world situation, or attitudes which inhibited choice and overall design, or even lethargy? There may be some truth in all these charges but I think the main explanation lies elsewhere. The problems were intractable. For much of the period the idea of breaking out of Churchill's Three Circles by opting for, say, an over-whelmingly European destiny simply did not mesh with the nature of Britain's real interests nor with political or popular sentiment. When the backcloth is, as it was for so long, one of economic decline and strain, policy is likely to shift and adjust constantly rather than be governed by some strategic vision which can be pursued regardless of these pressures. It was all just too difficult. I shall discuss in Chapter 8 attempts made in the last few years to define such a vision. In the period reviewed here the Holy Grail was not found but it was not for want of trying.

4

ADVISERS AND DECIDERS:

THE WAY FOREIGN POLICY IS MADE TODAY

The current problems of making foreign policy and their possible solutions cannot be sensibly discussed without first analysing the process by which policy is now made. Most of the academic descriptions of the process which I have read seem to me, as a former practitioner, rather unsatisfactory. But I make no criticism of that since access to recent archives is restricted and it is very difficult to compile an accurate account from secondary sources and such snippets as emerge from conversations with practitioners.

The formal process for making foreign policy is comparatively simple. The practical application of the process is often both complex and messy because the nature of foreign policy today is more complex than it was, because the pace of international events and media comment is quicker and the need for response more urgent, because the quantity and diversity of information available to policy-makers have greatly increased and because the process is operated by people. I shall deal first with the simple case – how foreign policy is made within the Foreign Office – and then introduce the complexities and messiness by describing the involvement of other actors. The process is not set in concrete. The role of the various players within it has fluctuated over the years and will continue to do so.

In 1998, the Foreign Office was organized hierarchically, with the following layers:

- Foreign and Commonwealth Secretary (Secretary of State)
- 4 Junior Ministers
- Permanent Under-Secretary
- 6 Deputy Under-Secretaries, each generally supervising a broad area of work, for example European Union and international economic affairs
- 18 Commands, each headed by a Director and each responsible for a geographical area of the world, for example the Americas, or a 'functional' subject, for example international security
- 74 Departments or Units, each covering a more specific area such as Latin America or a functional topic such as non-proliferation.[1]

Policy advice classically flows from an officer in one of the departments – for example, the desk officer for Argentina in the Latin American Department – by way of a written recommendation sent to the head of that department, perhaps then to the command director and onwards to a minister who decides whether to adopt the recommendation. The guiding principle is that officials advise while ministers decide. Many variations on the pattern are possible. In simple cases some links in the chain are bypassed. Then, policy can come from the top down as well as from the bottom up if, for example, a minister has independently decided what policy is to be followed in a particular case (though generally officials will be given the opportunity to advise against the prescription if they feel they should do so). It is in any case very common for policy advice to be stimulated not at desk-officer level but by a request from ministers for advice. Precisely how many officials consider a recommendation on its way to a minister depends on the importance of the issue, the number of officials with a direct interest in it, and the time available. In urgent situations the whole process is often short-circuited. The Foreign Secretary might simply call a meeting, hear advice and decide. Or a telephone call between two of the players might settle the matter. The common criticism that the organization of the Foreign Office is unduly hierarchical often assumes that advice always follows the hierarchical path contained in the formal organizational chart. That is not so.

There are three golden rules. First, each official in the chain must consider whether the issue need be transmitted higher. A prime consideration is whether the advice relates to the implementation of a policy already decided upon by ministers. If so, they can be spared another addition to their workload unless the new stage reached in implementation of the policy is so delicate in political or presentational terms that further ministerial authority is necessary. Second, whoever initiates advice must ensure that all in the Foreign Office (in this simple case) who have a direct interest in the matter are consulted and, if possible, their agreement obtained. Third, the written advice must be copied, as it is submitted up the chain, to all who need to know that the advice is being submitted (not quite the same as those having a direct interest in the subject). Again, where speed is necessary the process can be conducted orally.

But there are other players in the Foreign Office, not so far identified. Special advisers, usually political appointees, located in or near ministerial offices and typically two or three in number, will inject policy advice either directly to a minister or by way of comment on advice submitted by the official machine. Special advisers tend to concern themselves principally with the political or public impact of a potential policy decision. Officials with special responsibility for presentation of policy (the News and Information Departments) will pay particular attention to how and when policy developments should be publicly described and advise ministers accordingly. In recent years there has been great emphasis on incorporating presentational considerations into policy-making.

Those officials with general supervisory responsibilities for broad areas of policy, in particular the Permanent Under-Secretary and the six Deputy Under-Secretaries, will see copies of written advice as it is transmitted to ministers, and will from time to time comment from their broader perspective. But the hierarchical chain is not rigid. Senior officials may decide to initiate policy advice of their own and typically do so on issues of particular importance.

The bulk of advice which reaches ministers through this process is concerned with day-to-day policy-making. International events move quickly. Each morning brings a fresh crop of problems and situations to which a policy response is required. It is common for that response to be needed, fully cleared with all concerned, in time for the morning news conference conducted by the News Department, for ministerial lunch-time media interviews, for a parliamentary question or statement that afternoon, for a ministerial meeting suddenly convened or for ministerial red boxes which close some time in the early evening.

But there is also the planning machinery which is designed to produce policy advice with a longer perspective. In varying degrees all parts of the machine make planning for the future part of their routine work. But in reality this often has to take second place to the management of day-to-day policy-making. So the central place in planning is assigned to the Policy Planning Staff, a small group of officials who work under the direction of the Permanent Under-Secretary. In my day their principal papers were considered at a monthly meeting of the six Deputy Under-Secretaries under my chairmanship, in the so-called Policy Advisory Board. These meetings typically considered broad policy issues, usually straddling the

responsibilities of more than one Foreign Office department, and tended to look to the medium term, say, the
next five years. The papers would then often be for-
warded to the Foreign Secretary with the Board's policy
advice.

The same Board regularly examined a forecast of
future crises, compiled by the Policy Planning Staff,
which identified all likely crises around the world that
might affect British interests, described indicators which
would, when seen, suggest that a particular crisis was
likely to break and pointed to action which should be set
in hand to prevent the crises or mitigate their effects.
When a crisis occurred, the machine went into over-
drive, but since almost all crises involve other parts of
Whitehall I shall return to this point later.

The overseas network of diplomatic posts (221 in
1998) not only provides the Foreign Office and other
government departments with much of the information
on which policy advice is based but also contributes to
the advice itself by conveying recommendations as to the
course the government should follow.

The debate between overseas posts and London head-
quarters is a crucial part of the making of foreign policy.
The input of overseas missions varies widely from immediate analysis of, and urgent advice on, sudden crises and
events to deeper analysis of political and other trends in
the country concerned. If a terrorist incident involving
British citizens occurs in, say, a Latin American state the
first requirement of the policy-makers in London is a
report from the British ambassador on what has

happened, what is likely to happen and what action, in his or her view, the government should take. If a European Council meeting is in prospect, the views of the ambassador in Brussels on how the agenda items should be handled, what other member-states will seek to achieve, what British objectives should be and what result can reasonably be expected will have an important influence on the briefing supplied to the Prime Minister for the meeting. From time to time the ambassador in, say, Peking will provide medium-term analyses of how Chinese policies are likely to evolve and how British policies should be adjusted to influence them.

At the London end the practical manifestation of all this activity in posts across the world is the morning's crop of telegrams and e-mail messages, supplemented by a steady flow of letters and reports dealing with less immediate policy issues. As resources have diminished in London there has been some tendency to use overseas posts to provide policy advice direct to ministers rather than through the filter of London-based officials. There are dangers in this. Even the most competent posts can suffer 'localitis', the tendency to give more weight to the country on which they are reporting than it deserves, to be over-influenced by the views of host country and to take insufficient account of political and other factors at home. I would not think it wise to reduce much further the role of London officials in weighing, analysing and adjusting advice from overseas missions.

So much for the bare bones of the policy-making process within the Foreign Office. But a great deal of policy-making cannot be conducted by the Foreign Office alone. Aspects of foreign policy have always been of direct interest to some other government departments such as the Ministry of Defence and the Treasury. Nowadays, the number of Whitehall departments with a strong interest in some area of overseas activities has greatly increased. The current international agenda embraces issues of huge variety and is much less confined to the 'political' issues of foreign policy with which the Foreign Office was classically concerned. So a major element in the preparation of foreign policy advice is co-ordination between Whitehall departments. The question of which is the 'lead' department on an issue is usually readily apparent from past practice or the nature of the issue; and, if not, it must be quickly determined. If the Foreign Office is in the lead, as it is on most but by no means all foreign policy questions, it will seek to obtain the agreement of the other Whitehall depart-ments concerned on the content of policy advice before it is submitted to ministers. This can take any amount of time from a quick telephone or e-mail exchange to, if the subject is complex and large, a series of interdepart-mental meetings. The search for agreement between departments is sometimes criticized as inhibiting bold thinking and favouring the colourless compromise. It sometimes does. But its purpose is to make sure so far as possible that there is, at the end of the process, a policy which is endorsed by the government as a whole, not just an individual minister or department. Foreign policy is or should be the government's policy, not the policy of the

Foreign Office or some other department. The present government's emphasis on the need for 'joined-up' policy makes the same point.

Sometimes it is not possible to reach agreement between departments. Their respective ministers may then seek to do so in correspondence or by meeting informally. If success is still elusive, and if the issue is important enough (or sometimes if the issue is so important that a collective ministerial decision is needed in any case), the Cabinet machinery will come into play. One of the Cabinet ministerial committees concerned with overseas affairs, such as the Defence and Overseas Policy Committee or the Committee on European Questions, will be convened and the matter, hopefully and usually, decided. In practice, the Defence and Overseas Policy Committee does not meet very regularly, has tended to do so only when there is interdepartmental disagreement which cannot be resolved and has generally confined itself to rather narrow issues such as a defence contract. The Committee on European Questions has met much more frequently, largely because of the volume of European Union business that straddles the interests of Whitehall departments. For it would be wrong to think of the central co-ordinating machinery as being concerned only to resolve matters where there is disagreement between departments. There are units in the Cabinet Office, for example the overseas and defence section of the Secretariat and the European Unit, which were created to ensure effective co-ordination of government policy in their areas. The European Unit has come

to play a particularly important role in co-ordinating
the network of official committees which deal with
European issues and in advising the Prime Minister on
the handling of these issues. For completeness, I should
add that Cabinet ministerial committees are often under-
pinned by committees of officials which prepare
recommendations for ministerial consideration.

At the apex of the system is the Cabinet which might
in theory be involved in major foreign policy issues. In
practice, it rarely is. An issue of great sensitivity, such as
the dispatch of British troops to a war zone, or of very
considerable political delicacy, such as qualified majority
voting in the European Union, would normally be discussed in Cabinet. But it is quite wrong to think of
Cabinet as being frequently involved in the making of
foreign policy, even at the strategic level. That has not
been the case for many years now. There has been a practice whereby the Foreign Secretary informs the weekly
Cabinet meeting of the state of play on two or three international issues but typically this has not led to discussion.

One other element of the central co-ordinating
machinery should be mentioned, the Joint Intelligence
Committee (JIC) and the Assessment Staff which under-
pins it. The role of the JIC is described by Sir Percy
Cradock, a former chairman, as one of monitoring and
giving early warning of the development of direct or
indirect foreign threats to British interests whether political, military or economic.[2] Its task is the assessment of
information and situations and to some extent the prediction of developments. It does not give policy advice

but its assessments frequently stimulate policy advice from those responsible for policy-making and affect the content of that advice. In crisis situations the JIC and/or the Assessment Staff move into high gear, not uncommonly meeting two or three times a day to produce assessments of a fast-moving situation such as war in the Gulf or a terrorist incident involving British interests. Special arrangements are made for continuous inter-departmental exchanges while the crisis lasts and the Foreign Office may well open and staff its emergency rooms.

Much ink has been devoted to describing the role of the Prime Minister and the staff of No. 10 Downing Street in foreign policy. It is in fact difficult to produce a description which fits the facts accurately at any given time. Historically, much has depended on the predilection of the particular Prime Minister in office and his or her relationship with, in particular, the Foreign Secretary. Yet it is undeniably the case that, whatever the personal interest of the modern Prime Minister in foreign affairs, the extent to which he or she is *obliged* to become involved has greatly increased. The formal requirements to attend meetings of the European Council, the G8 summits and the Commonwealth Heads of Government meetings, together with the semi-commitment to attend regular bilateral meetings with other Prime Ministers, notably those of European member-states, lock the incumbent inescapably into a considerable amount of foreign affairs activity. The intertwining of European Union and domestic affairs and the high political salience of much EU activity also ensure plenty of demands on the Prime Minister's time.

Even in my own period as Private Secretary to the Prime Minister for foreign and defence affairs in the early 1980s, the involvement of No. 10 in major overseas issues was close. My impression is that it has increased since then. The Private Secretary post in question was upgraded in the late 1980s and has since been under-pinned with another official, and there is other evidence pointing in the same direction. It has long been the prac-tice for much foreign policy business to be conducted between the Prime Minister and the Foreign Secretary at regular bilateral meetings, and the private offices of the two ministers are in constant contact throughout the average working day.

This account has so far been confined to the process within Whitehall. But there are many actors outside Whitehall who affect policy-making. The consensus of those who have written about the subject is that Parliament's influence on foreign policy is limited, that area of government being regarded largely as the prov-ince of the executive. I believe that to be true up to a point. The first exception is European Union-related issues. Given their often high political profile govern-ments and oppositions are obliged to pay attention to the spread of parliamentary opinion. Second, in a situ-ation of crisis, the views of members of Parliament will often affect the content of policy-making. In the case of Bosnia in recent years, an assessment of what Parliament would find tolerable in the way of British involvement played its role in determining the parameters of policy. Nor shall I easily forget the dramatic and angry atmosphere in the Commons chamber on 3 April 1982 when I was present in the Officials' Box to watch the then Prime Minister open a debate on Argentina's invasion of the Falkland Islands, described in her memoirs as the most difficult she ever had to face.[3] But in calmer times the direct influence of Parliament on the content of policy is not strong. Foreign affairs Question Time requires serious preparation by ministers and officials but it occurs only monthly and is not often well attended. Debates on foreign affairs are relatively few and, except where a politically charged European Union issue or a crisis involving British troops is to the fore, do not fill much of the chamber. Correspondence between Foreign Office ministers and members of Parliament is bulky and receives much attention. The Select Committee on Foreign Affairs has grown in prominence in the years since its establishment, has travelled widely as part of its investigations, and has produced a series of reports on policy issues, but has often revealed its frustration that its policy advice has not made a greater impact.

The development of political co-operation within the European Union, in particular the attempt to construct a Common Foreign and Security Policy, has certainly impinged on the policy process in the Foreign Office, substantially increasing the workload of ministers and officials alike. It involves the Foreign Secretary in regular meetings with his opposite numbers in the countries of the Union. An almost automatic response to an international crisis is the urgent convening of foreign ministers in a European capital. The Political Director of the Foreign Office follows a similar rhythm of meetings with his European colleagues and is one of the busiest of its senior officials, spending, like the Foreign Secretary, an unreasonable amount of his or her life in the air and in hotels. A secure communications link directly connects the foreign ministries of the member-states. Desk officers deal directly with opposite numbers in the Union, both outside and within the large array of working groups which has been constituted to deal with specific areas of foreign policy work. The practice of political co-operation extends across the world. In most capitals there are regular meetings of the member-states and Commission representatives and the technique of joint reporting is by now pretty well developed.

Thus there is a very sizeable bureaucratic structure designed to improve the co-ordination of foreign policy-making in the European Union. The limitations of the Common Foreign and Security Policy will be discussed in a later chapter. The point to note here is that it has become a significant dimension in the policy-making process in London. In judging policy advice in areas where the CFSP is active, officials will be inclined to consider which policy is likely to command agreement with member-states. But the golden rule still applies: the British representative in any meeting convened in the political co-operation machinery must ensure that the outcome conforms with the policy decisions of

British ministers or reserve the position until the matter can be discussed with them.

The European Union is only one, albeit the most important, of the very many multilateral organizations of which the United Kingdom is a member. A few of them, notably the United Nations, especially its Security Council, and NATO, make an impact on the process similar in some ways to that of the Union's political co-operation machinery.

There is a separate category of outside actors who have no formal role in foreign policy-making but whose informal role is significant and in some cases growing in importance: business, non-governmental organizations, academics, think-tanks and the media.

A common theme of the formal reviews of overseas representation discussed in the last chapter was that more emphasis should be placed by government on support for British business in its overseas activities. In general, and certainly in the last ten to fifteen years, this area of policy has had high priority in Whitehall and in overseas diplomatic posts. British firms have several channels through which to convey their views on policy to government and the policy-makers are now usually very conscious of the need to ensure that overseas policies actively encourage, or are at least consistent with, the promotion of the country's international economic and commercial interests (or, where this is not the case, that there are good reasons why it cannot be so). The Foreign Office itself, which conducts export and investment promotion activity jointly with the Department of Trade and Industry, has a closer relationship with British business than at any time in its history. Commercial work is a high priority for the majority of overseas diplomatic missions. Where it is not, this is because the country concerned is not a priority for British business. As Permanent Under-Secretary I chaired a joint panel of top business representatives and senior FCO officials which met periodically to exchange views on a business-related agenda. But the contacts with firms are too varied and numerous to describe here in full.

Exchanges with non-governmental organizations about foreign policy are an area of increasing salience. During the period of my own career the role and status of non-governmental organizations were transformed. My first job in the Foreign Office in 1964 was that of desk officer for human rights, together with a number of other issues which had limited prominence in foreign policy at the time such as the status of women, population issues, social questions, narcotics and statistics (the rationale for linking these subjects was that they were each the concern of one of the functional commissions of the UN Economic and Social Council). NGOs were then seen, rightly or wrongly, largely as campaigning organizations whose main function was to criticize government and who were therefore to be kept at a certain distance. Some thirty years later, as Permanent Under-Secretary, I invited the heads of seventeen NGOs to a morning of discussion at the Foreign Office which concentrated on the objectives of our foreign policy. This is but one illustration of the much closer links which the department now has with these organizations. Many of them, while naturally still critical of government policy where it impedes their objectives, often see value in trying to enlist the co-operation of government in the pursuit of their aims. Some have developed expertise and knowledge in particular areas of the world. When they are prepared to share this information it can be of real value to the policy-makers. I think, however, that there is still much scope to expand this relationship to the benefit of government and the organizations concerned. I shall refer later to recent steps taken by the Foreign Office in this direction.

There is a continuous effort, too, to engage with academic experts from the universities and organizations with a special interest in overseas policy such as the Royal Institute for International Affairs and the International Institute for Strategic Studies. The Foreign Office policy planning staff and the research cadre hold regular exchanges with such experts and many of the individual departments do their best to draw on external expertise when the pressure of daily work permits. But the activity is probably not so well targeted to policy-making ends as, for example, in the United States, nor is there the same facility for academics to move in and out of government which has made such a strong impact on policy-thinking in America. The academic input into policy-thinking is at its most effective in direct discussion with the policy-makers. The latter will normally have little time for extensive reading of academic work. (I fear that the resources devoted in academic circles to international relations theory are unlikely to have much

influence on the practitioner, largely because the products seem rather remote from the practical business of
conducting foreign policy, though that of course may not
be the principal objective of these studies.)

In Britain the think-tanks established either independently or by the political parties have devoted most of
their attention to domestic policy. I did not find them a
particularly fertile source of ideas on foreign policy
during my own career though they no doubt had some
indirect effect to the extent that their ideas influenced the
foreign policy content of the manifestos and other documents of the political parties which, when in
government, implemented them at least in part.

Finally, among external players, the media. A full analysis of the impact of the modern media on the
policy-making process would require a separate book. In
contrast to the earlier periods of British foreign policy
discussed in the previous chapter, the most obvious effect
today of the large and insistent presence of television,
radio and the press is the amount of time which the
policy-makers feel obliged to devote to presentation. I
can recall occasions when the Foreign Secretary has spent
several hours of the working day preparing for and giving
media interviews of one kind and another. There have
been times, indeed, when strategic policy discussion has
been cancelled to make time for the media. While good
public presentation of foreign policy is important, and
sometimes vital, the fact is that time spent with the media
is largely time lost to policy-thinking.

That effect apart, the actual impact of the media on

policy-making is harder to assess. The extent to which individual press articles or television programmes actually influence the minds of policy-makers is difficult to gauge. Sometimes policy is adjusted to avoid a critical media response but the adjustment is usually more at the margins than at the substance of policy. Nor is such trimming necessarily a bad thing if the objective is to deliver public support for policy. The greater risk is that media pressure may distort the substance of policy by producing strong public demands for action on a particular issue when that action would be inconsistent with the best available assessment of what is necessary to pursue the British interest in the issue. The immense power of the television screen can often create such pressure through, for example, horrifying pictures of casualties in civil war or famine. The calls for the government to do something become insistent. It may be right to respond with action but it may not. For such media coverage is usually partial, concentrating perhaps on one civil war, where reporters happen to be present, but ignoring several raging elsewhere. Then the constant portrayal of disasters distorts the overall image of foreign policy. As the present Foreign Secretary, Robin Cook, told a seminar recently, 'You will never see on the prime five-minute slot at the top of the television news programme: "Great Breakthrough by Foreign Office Officials in Preventing Conflict from Breaking Out".'[4]

But in general I think those who argue that the media nowadays make, as well as report, policy greatly exaggerate. I suspect that the media do have significant impact on the making of domestic policy and perhaps on foreign economic policy. But it is not my experience that other aspects of foreign policy have often been changed by media coverage alone. A prominent journalist who recently studied the role of media coverage in the prevention of conflict believes that 'Ultimately, despite all the bleating, the vital national interests and strategic assessments of governments hold sway over emotions' and concludes that beyond the mere fact of reporting conflicts, or signs pointing to a looming conflict, there are significant limits on the influence of the media.[5]

None of which means that the media cannot be a useful source of information and ideas for policy-makers. It is almost always valuable to exchange information and thoughts with journalists experienced in reporting international developments, within the limits that the professional rules impose on both parties. Embassies across the world have benefited in this way. But good foreign policy-making has to be based on the most reliable, most illuminating and most professional information that can be obtained. That will usually come from the mass of reporting which reaches Whitehall every day from the overseas diplomatic missions. For, when they are doing their job properly, they will have access to sources and information which are not available to the media, especially in more closed societies, and should have a background of deep immersion in a country's affairs which enables them to report to their government with perspective and insight. The sources of information available to policy-makers are nowadays almost endless. Clearly, as many of them as possible should be used but there is no substitute for reports from those government officials serving abroad whose professional role and duty it is to report and analyse in an unbiased and diligent way, not in order to make headlines but to aid good policy decisions at the centre.

Chapter 2 of this book records the view of many outside observers that a constant weakness in British foreign policy-making since 1945 has been the failure to set clear objectives. But today objectives are set and published regularly in a source which, so far as I can see, has not been much used in academic writing, namely the annual reports by the Foreign Office (and other government departments) to Parliament on the government's expenditure plans. This series, which in its present form dates from 1991, ought to be a valuable source of material for outside observers. The 1998 Report by the Foreign Office prints the Department's Mission Statement of 12 May 1997 (which I discuss in more detail in Chapter 8) and defines the general aim of policy as 'to promote the national interest of the United Kingdom and to contribute to a strong world community'.[6] It then lists eight objectives:

- to ensure the security of the UK; and to promote international peace and stability;
- to improve, through international action, economic opportunities for a prosperous UK;
- to improve the quality of life world-wide; and to develop a strong international community;

- to increase the impact of and respect for British foreign policy and values;
- to ensure the UK plays a strong role in a strong Europe, responsive to people's needs;
- to ensure the protection of British citizens abroad;
- to ensure efficient and effective implementation of entry-clearance arrangements; and
- to ensure the security of UK overseas territories, promote their prosperity and uphold sustainable development and good government.

The report further lists the ways in which each objective is to be pursued. For a complete picture of the government's overseas objectives it is necessary to consult the annual reports of all other Whitehall departments which have international activities such as the Ministry of Defence, the Treasury, the Department of Environment, Transport and the Regions, the Department of International Development and many others. Each department also delivers to Parliament in the same document its assessment of how far the stated objectives of the previous year have been attained.

The Foreign Office, like other departments, has long used the technique of 'management by objectives'. The general objectives described above are 'cascaded' down in more detailed form to commands and departments in London and to overseas missions, and eventually to individuals. Every British diplomat has written objectives. I had them myself as Permanent Under-Secretary.

So, whatever the case in the more distant past, the claim that objectives for foreign policy are not clearly set has not been sustainable for many years. Of course, there is still room for discussion about the validity and consistency of those objectives. They are open to the criticism that they are the product of a bureaucratic exercise linked to annual expenditure decisions and are not necessarily uppermost in the minds of the policy-makers when foreign policy speeches are made and specific issues are pursued. It is also one thing to state an objective but quite another to devote adequate time and resources to pursuing it. Some objectives may prove to be entirely declaratory in nature. It is also the case that annual reports deal with only one kind of objective. To state the precise aims of Britain in each individual country would cause embarrassment and go a long way to defeat their purpose (the same applies to, for example, Japanese or German objectives in Britain). Nor is it sensible to reveal negotiating objectives. Nevertheless, it is evident that one of the charges levelled at the policy-makers, and described earlier, no longer holds water.

Any written description of the policy-making process is likely to leave the impression that it is more orderly than it is in practice. On any working day there are hundreds of telegrams from overseas missions to be dealt with, together with a mass of information from other sources. The official who has only one problem to deal with at any one time is the lucky exception. The process of preparing advice is often disrupted by demands from elsewhere – from Downing Street, from a Foreign Office minister, from the rest of Whitehall and so on. In fast-moving situations, advice is often re-tailored more than once as fresh information arrives. When the advice is ready a minister has to find time to deal with it but ministerial life is even more open to disruption as ministerial meetings are suddenly convened or media comment becomes urgent or an emergency debate is scheduled in Parliament. More ministerial decisions are taken in the backs of cars, in airport lounges, even in bathrooms than is good for anyone's digestion, but this is often unavoidable.

Nor is policy advice the only activity in which the Foreign Office is engaged. Far from it. I have commented earlier on the heavy load of management tasks which occupy most officials some of the time and some all of the time. There are foreign and British visitors to be seen and endless briefs to be prepared. And much time is taken up in travelling for a wide variety of purposes, for example to attend European Union and other international meetings. Conflicting demands and tight deadlines often produce an atmosphere which is anything but serene and hardly conducive to clear and measured thought. But this 'messiness' is, largely unavoidably, part of Foreign Office life and somehow the best possible policy-thinking has to be made to emerge from it.

5

NOT WHAT IT WAS:

THE NATURE OF FOREIGN POLICY TODAY

It is not just the increased complexity of the policy-making process which inhibits the construction of sound policy. The very substance of foreign policy is much more complex than it once was. Half a century ago my predecessors could compile their weighty memoranda of advice to the Foreign Secretary on the assumption that Britain had sufficient autonomous power to implement a desired policy, or at least that it would be necessary to persuade only a handful of other countries of its merit. But now the global system is thoroughly interdependent. Britain is incomparably more reliant on the behaviour of a multitude of other states and non-state actors to secure its aims. Many policies have long had to be pursued through multilateral organizations where the outcome of negotiation is uncertain. International and domestic affairs are more closely enmeshed. Globalization – the rapid growth of traffic of many different kinds across state borders without the intervention of government – has limited still further the power of states to take independent decisions. New issues of a kind hardly contemplated by the policy-makers of the early post-war period have risen to prominence on the international agenda and presented new conceptual and organizational problems. The technical complexity of the issues which the policy-makers address is markedly greater. Since the end of the Cold War increasing reluctance to use military power as an instrument of foreign policy, particularly where it may involve casualties, has coincided with the multiplication of civil wars and 'failed states' which might appear to require the use of armed international intervention to restore stability. Most of these trends are not new but their evolution over time and their gathering momentum have markedly changed the character of foreign policy.

The interdependence of states in the international system and the growth of multilateral diplomacy are two sides of the same coin. The sustained use of massive military power by a single country to pursue its policy objectives is increasingly rare. Only the United States currently has the capacity for it, but the Americans have a clear preference for acting in coalition with others. For lesser powers, a coalition is well nigh indispensable for serious military action. NATO provides a permanent coalition for its members. Where it cannot act, *ad hoc* coalitions are nowadays generally sought. In the economic field the pursuit of many goals has long and necessarily been conducted on a basis of international negotiation and co-operation. Commonly, a priority task for British policy-makers when launching a new policy initiative is to assemble a credible grouping of other countries which have an interest in pursuing it.

This does not mean that there are no areas left for autonomous action. Britain still conducts most of its bilateral relationships with other countries round the world at least partly on an independent basis. There is never a shortage of bilateral problems between Britain and individual states to be addressed. It is not hard to recall recent cases where Britain has been the prime mover in diplomatic action, naturally seeking the support of other countries but not unduly influenced by their thinking. The negotiation of the Sino-British agreement on the future of Hong Kong (1984) is one such example.

But for many years the success or otherwise of British foreign policy has been in large part due to the use made of international organizations. Leaving aside the special case of the European Union, in 1998 Britain planned to spend some £90 million in contributions to the United Nations (Regular Budget), the Commonwealth Secretariat, the Council of Europe, the Western European Union, the OECD and NATO, and was spending well over three times that amount on subscriptions to a large array of UN specialized agencies and other organizations and UN peace-keeping operations.[1] This deep engagement with multilateral organizations affects British policy-makers from the bottom, where contact with opposite numbers in other countries and participation in international meetings are the bread and butter of diplomacy, up through the system to the top where the Prime Minister, as mentioned in the last chapter, regularly attends a large number of summits each year. Britain has the opportunity to play, and is often expected by the international community to play, a leading role in this kind of diplomacy because of its status as a permanent member of the UN Security Council, its possession of one of the world's largest economies, its relative weight in the European Union and the special reputation of its armed forces and other assets. Much effort has to be expended on preparation for international gatherings, on assessment of the likely objectives and tactics of others and on lobbying, often world-wide, to attempt to persuade others to support the British position at the meetings themselves. Then success in such multilateral negotiations depends in part on the quality of briefings supplied to the British representative, in part on the tactical skills and powers of advocacy deployed on the day.

There has never been a clear separation of overseas and domestic policy. Foreign and defence policies have always largely depended on economic capacity. Public opinion helps to shape the parameters of a country's international activity. Domestic reactions to an overseas event sometimes oblige a foreign policy response. These are constant factors. But foreign and domestic policies are now more closely interwoven than in any earlier period. This is in part a function of interdependence. In a world where Britain is more dependent on other countries than hitherto, where modern communications have shrunk the world and brought events into living-rooms in real time, where an economic decision in the United States or Japan or Brazil can be seen to have immediate implications for jobs in Britain, the world matters more to British citizens. As Andrew Marr puts it, perhaps with some exaggeration, 'The British, in short, happened to other people. Now the world happens to Britain.'[2] This is not to say that most foreign policy is of interest to British public opinion. Media surveys tend to suggest the opposite. But the potential for a strong domestic reaction to an overseas development is always there and the policy-makers must factor that potential into their thinking.

British membership of the European Union has greatly intensified the interaction of domestic and foreign policy, to the point where it is often difficult to determine what is domestic and what international, as one practitioner has pointed out:

> An EC regulation with direct legislative effect in the member states is to all intents and purposes domestic law in each of them . . . there is now hardly an important area of national economic life . . . which has not been subject to international negotiation, legislation, or at least co-ordination and co-operation in Brussels.[3]

The British standard of living depends ever more closely on the Union's internal and external economic policies and its success or failure in external trade negotiations. As discussed in the previous chapter, the Common Foreign and Security Policy is an important dimension of foreign policy work. If the process of European integration continues at its present rate the line between domestic and foreign policy will become even more blurred.

The radical changes in the world brought about by the end of the Cold War also contributed to this general process. The removal of the West's major security preoccupation allowed other foreign policy concerns, of more direct interest to domestic constituencies, to come to the fore. 'In a world of geo-economics . . . the balance of trade was just as important as the balance of terror and counting . . . jobs was as critical as counting Moscow's warheads.'[4] In many Western countries the promotion of overseas trade became for a time practically synonymous with foreign policy. No longer was reference to the Soviet threat available to deflect special-issue groups from pressing their aims. Non-governmental organizations and other domestic groups exerted more influence on the policies of governments and liaised more effectively with counterpart bodies in other countries.

The concept of 'globalization' encapsulates most of these trends but more besides. As national economic enterprises are increasingly replaced by multinational ones so economic production becomes as much an international as a domestic phenomenon. Britain has been conspicuously successful in recent years in attracting inward investment. Substantial areas of economic activity are now effectively owned by foreign corporations. But Britain is also the largest investor overseas after the United States and in 1998 spent about US\$130 billion acquiring foreign companies.[5] Not only capital but also labour migrates more freely across international borders. International communications are increasingly integrated and governments are less and less able to control the flow of information from one part of the world to another. The beneficial effects of globalization are accompanied by undesirable consequences – for example, greater capacity for terrorists and criminals of other kinds to operate internationally and increased illicit trade in drugs and weapons.

The policy-makers are confronted with a rapidly changing agenda. The memoirs of recent British Foreign Secretaries show that they spent little time dealing with other than the classical political and security issues of foreign policy, or at least that other issues did not weigh sufficiently with them to merit extensive treatment in their writing. This is unlikely to be so in future. As Douglas Hurd observes, 'National and international institutions will increasingly wrestle with the problems of the environment, climatic change, drugs, population growth and migration, and pollution of all kinds.'[6] Most of these so-called 'new issues' of foreign policy are in reality not new in substance. Their novelty lies in the fact that they have become threats of significant dimension to the well-being of the world's population; that in practically all cases they seem likely to grow in strength rather than diminish; that they are pre-eminently problems which can be tackled *only* by serious international co-operation since they recognize no frontiers; and thus they have become issues of international diplomacy. They pose particular difficulties for policy-makers because, while they have the potential to cause massive harm, they do not, with the possible exception of migration, yet have the immediacy of more familiar challenges to security and prosperity such as the outbreak of hostilities or the disruption of trade, and because predictions as to when and how they are likely to impinge on a state's interests are even more uncertain than in the case of more conventional foreign policy problems. They are also peculiarly difficult for politicians, naturally preoccupied with short electoral cycles, to address.

There is one other feature of contemporary foreign policy which requires fundamental policy-thinking, though it is less clear how prominent a feature it will be, namely the apparently changing attitudes to the use of force in international relations. Conventionally, the knowledge that a state possessed the military capacity to pursue or at least to defend its interests and objectives greatly increased the chances of the aims of its foreign policy being achieved. In theory this is clearly still so. But in a series of recent cases, for example in Iraq and in the conflicts in former Yugoslavia, a growing reluctance to incur casualties has been evident, particularly on the part of the United States. Aerial bombardment, with its limited risk of injury to those carrying it out, is acceptable. The use of ground forces in a combat role is increasingly unacceptable. While a military strategy of this kind has its uses, it looks increasingly ineffective as a way of restoring stability to unstable areas.

Conflict is as prevalent now as in the past. At any given time there are numerous civil wars in progress across the world, usually in 'failed states' where the machinery to govern and maintain order has simply collapsed. Traditional concepts of peace-keeping now seem ineffective. But alternatives have not been found. This may be a temporary situation. Possibly, events will oblige the United States and others to revert in the future to more conventional applications of military power and the current reluctance to risk lives will be overcome. But if this proves not to be the case, then the nature of foreign policy will be radically altered in this respect as well. There is already talk of 'powerless politics' where the United States cannot oblige even small states to do what it wants, and neither they nor the European Union can persuade the two halves of Cyprus to unite.[7]

The text of this book was completed shortly after the end of the NATO campaign in Kosovo in the summer of 1999. Many of the issues described above were the subject of active public debate during the weeks of the campaign. The initial reluctance of NATO to use ground forces was a matter of considerable controversy. The apparent readiness at a later stage to use such troops may have been a factor in inducing the Serbian leadership to seek a settlement. But only time will tell whether the Kosovo episode indicates a permanent return to a more traditional view of the role of force in international affairs.

In the 1990s there has been much talk of preventive diplomacy, action to forestall situations which in some way threaten the interests of one or more states or of the world community. This has, of course, been one of the functions of diplomacy since its creation. But the concept has developed novel force because the world community now has in theory a greater capacity to intervene with economic and technical assistance and to mount peace-making and peace-keeping operations; because the inhibitions on intervention in the affairs of another country, once famously protected by Article 2(7) of the United Nations Charter, have generally weakened; because the rapid transmission of information gives clearer and earlier warning of situations which may demand intervention; and because the removal of the all-pervading superpower confrontation of the Cold War and the emergence of new states have allowed many hidden tensions to develop into conflict or near-conflict.

The great difficulty about preventive diplomacy of the new kind is that, to be effective, decisive and expensive action is usually needed at a time when it is difficult to convince those who decide policy and control budgets that that action is justifiable in political and financial terms. By the time the need for action is compellingly clear the best moment for it may well have gone. This kind of diplomacy often needs much clarity of vision and political courage and its difficulties are often not well understood. Shrill demands that 'something must be done' are common. But questions as to how, when, at what cost and at what price to other areas of government policy are less readily answered.

Confronted with this rapidly changing international environment, with a world where so much happens that is outside the control of government, where economic well-being and even political stability can seem to be affected as much by the decisions of international firms as by those who make official policy and where many of the 'big' issues such as climate change appear to have little to do with foreign policy as traditionally conceived, it is sometimes argued that foreign policy is a thing of the past, that it now has no useful role. But this is misguided, for at least two reasons. First, the decline in the power of governments to affect events is exaggerated. As *The Economist* argued in a recent article, state involvement in domestic economies is growing not shrinking and the proportion of a country's income which governments spend is rising. Since 1980 public spending in the big economies has increased on average from 36 per cent to 40 per cent. It is still governments that set the framework for economic action, domestically and internationally.[8] It is still states that provide security for their citizens. And the burgeoning debate about national identity cannot conceal the fact that for most people their primary loyalty, among political entities, is to the country to which they belong nor the fact that the world is still largely organized on the basis of nation-states.

Second, the world may be bewilderingly complex but it is still there. Countries need the capacity to understand it and to pursue and defend their interests within it. The likelihood of events elsewhere impinging on the security and welfare of Britain is greater than it was. If Britain's ability to get what it wants through the exercise of power is diminished, then there is a premium on the conduct of foreign policy by other means. There is no option but to pursue the most effective and vigorous diplomacy, directed at well-conceived objectives, that resources and talents permit. But the organization and methods employed need to evolve as rapidly as the new features of the international environment emerge.

In Whitehall the evolution has been considerable. When I became a diplomat in 1960, the most prestigious departments in the Foreign Office were the so-called geographical departments, those that dealt with specific areas of the world such as the Middle East or the Soviet and Eastern European countries. The great men (and they were nearly all men) were those who advised during the Arab-Israeli wars of 1967 and 1973 or who developed policy towards the Soviet world in the 1970s or who analysed events in China and their possible impact on Hong Kong. Today, reflecting interdependence and multilateralism, the largest departments, where the most ambitious and able want to work, are the 'functional' departments, those that deal not with a geographical area but with a subject or group of subjects, such as the two European Union departments dealing with external and internal EU affairs, the International Security Department, dealing among other things with NATO, and the United Nations Department.

Then, as the 'new issues' have moved up the agenda, so other 'functional' departments have become more important. In 1964, I was *the* Human Rights Officer in the Foreign Office and I cannot say that much attention was paid to my work (it was at that time that a Labour Foreign Secretary initially decided that the United

Kingdom would *not* ratify the United Nations Convention on the Elimination of Racial Discrimination). Today, a whole department of eleven diplomats plus supporting staff handles human rights policy, a clear demonstration of the salience of human rights issues in contemporary foreign policy and of the need to bring human rights considerations to bear on other aspects of policy. One of my last acts as Permanent Under-Secretary in 1997 was to establish a Global Issues Command, grouping previously dispersed subjects such as the environment, science, energy, economic relations, aviation and maritime matters, as well as human rights and UN affairs, with the aim of providing a better focus on frontier-cutting issues of this kind. We created a separate Command to deal with drugs, international crime and terrorism because these issues needed a different operational response and involved a discrete group of Whitehall actors.

The international sections of many primarily domestic departments have expanded over the last two decades mainly because of the impact of European business on their areas of work but also because of the increasing interplay of domestic and international affairs. Most of the global issues discussed above demand and get close co-operation across Whitehall. Drugs and international crime bring together the Foreign Office, the Home Office, the intelligence agencies, the police and others. Environmental issues impinge in one way or another on most Whitehall departments. But the emphasis on multilateralism and global issues should not obscure the fact that much foreign policy is still concerned with the conduct of bilateral relations between individual states and with response to specific situations or problems in specific countries. The geographical departments still have their role. It is from them that most of the advice will come on the handling of overseas issues which impinge most on the public consciousness: Bosnia, the Arab-Israeli dispute, events in the Gulf, civil war in Africa, Kashmir, China, political turbulence in south-east Asia. And it is the diplomatic missions on the ground that will provide the basic advice on the classic security and political issues as they affect the countries to which they are accredited, and on the impact of 'functional' issues on these countries and on political, social and economic developments in individual states across the world.

How, in today's world, can we assess whether a country's general foreign policy, or policy on specific international issues, is successful or not?

In the first case – the general one – it is difficult to do so if there is no overall public statement of a government's foreign policy aims against which to measure specific achievements or failures. Without such a statement, the assessment becomes unduly subjective. The assessor has to decide personally whether the results of foreign policy actions were intentional and, if so, whether the intentions were valid in terms of national interest or some other criteria, and in the light of that whether the consequence of actions represented success, failure or something in between. However, as I shall argue in more detail in Chapter 8, such statements of overall aims do now exist in respect of Britain.

The starting point for an assessment could well be the Foreign Office's annual reports to Parliament. The 1998 Report contains, as mentioned above, not only a clear statement of objectives but also five pages describing the specific areas in which those objectives are regarded as having been achieved. A critical assessment would no doubt consider whether any important objectives have been omitted, seek to analyse the quality of the objectives in terms of their relevance to British interests and their internal consistency, and examine the proclaimed achievements in some detail. It would also consider whether there have been significant cases of failure to achieve objectives since these are unlikely to be highlighted in official reports. It would be right, too, to distinguish between aims which are purely declaratory in nature and those which are seriously pursued by sustained diplomacy. For it is perfectly possible to have a 'policy' on an issue without, for whatever reason, devoting time and resources to its pursuit. In this case policy is no more than a statement of attitude or position. Also, policy is not always predetermined but is sometimes a description given after the event to a bundle of statements and actions which emerged in an *ad hoc* fashion as a situation developed. Then, as I have suggested earlier, it would be necessary to take into account the international activity of other Whitehall departments as described in their own annual reports to Parliament. Finally, it would be surprising if the actual pattern of international events during a particular year conveniently matched the objectives set out by government at its commencement. It would be more than likely that an unforeseen situation had suddenly developed and come to dominate foreign policy for part or all of the year in question.

But with all those cautions the material does exist publicly for an assessment of the overall effectiveness of British foreign policy during a prescribed period. If the established objectives are clearly relevant to British interests and are in large part achieved then it would be fair to describe the outcome as 'successful'.

It is perhaps more difficult to assess the merits of policy on specific issues. More detailed analysis is needed and some of the necessary material will often not be publicly available because it is confidential in nature and the archives which contain it are closed. But in principle the methodology would be similar to that suggested above. Consider the stated objectives and examine how far they were achieved. In a fast-moving international crisis, however, it may be difficult to establish the policy objectives that were being pursued at any given time. While it might seem elementary that clear aims should be formulated at the outset, it is often only as the crisis unfolds and its causes and implications are studied over time that it is possible to decide with any precision what they should be.

When the former republic of Yugoslavia disintegrated, and fighting broke out in Bosnia, should priority have been given to the containment of hostilities so that instability did not spread through the Balkans more generally, or to enforcing a cessation of hostilities so that loss of life was minimized, or to preserving the unity of NATO, or to promoting the negotiation of a political solution aimed at providing a framework for future stability, and, if the last, should that solution have been based on an integrated Bosnian state or on the broad separation of mutually hostile communities? How big was the British interest in any of these things and what means did Britain have of pursuing any of these priorities? Policymakers could not reasonably be expected to have a ready answer to such questions but typically spent hours and days in examining them while all the time dealing with the immediate requirements of day-to-day management of the issues. Bosnia was 'intellectually and ethically tangled . . . there was no clear leader of the efforts, no master plan . . . each country formed a view and then tried to work with others. We tried not to be entirely pragmatic . . . we were forever trying to cut through the tangle by applying tests of principle.'[9] These comments by Douglas Hurd, Foreign Secretary at the time, illustrate some of the complexities of the issue.

In this and similar cases such as the Kosovo crisis of 1999 the limits on autonomous British action will be plain. The eventual policy pursued is more likely to be the policy of the European Union or NATO or the UN Security Council than the independent policy of Britain. So the eventual assessment of the merits of British policy will essentially be a matter of tracing and evaluating the British contribution to policy-making in the relevant multilateral organization. Thus, there is little alternative to a detailed case study, compiled after the event and using the best material available. Only such a study would show convincingly how effective British policy had been – by which time, probably, the real world would have moved on to some more urgent preoccupation. Even the most carefully researched study would encounter the difficulty of reconstructing the actual circumstances in which policy was made. So often exhaustive accounts, written well after the event, fall into the trap of hindsight, take little or no account of the other issues which were on the policy-makers' minds, do not consider whether decisions were reached in orderly circumstances, with time available for proper reflection, or, as is frequently the case, under great pressure of time and events and perhaps at the end of an immensely busy day or night when the policy-makers, being people, were tired. It is often a messy and ragged process, the true nature of which is very hard to capture when looking back.

In Chapter 7 I consider the case of Australia which in recent years has brought about a major shift in its foreign policy orientation, primarily designed to maximize its economic interests in Asian markets. I regard that example as a good case study of success, from which useful lessons can be drawn. The fact that the Australian government's thinking was so public and so subject to public debate makes analysis a good deal easier than in other cases.

There is a sense in which British policy-making *ought* to be successful given the quality of the institutions involved. After all, we have a democratic system that ensures that governments have to answer to the electorate at least every five years. The mistakes typically made by authoritarian regimes which, free of checks and balances, persist in misguided policy long after it has any justification, are unlikely to occur in Britain. Parliament and public opinion are there between elections to question policy and constrain excess. The dedication of ministers and officials to the job compares impressively with that found in many other countries. The quality of information available to the policy-maker from overt and covert sources is higher than in most comparable countries. So if the product of the policy-making process is less good than it ought to be the explanation is unlikely to be found in the fundamental quality of the institutions involved but elsewhere.

A detailed analysis of the extent to which British foreign policy has been well made in recent years lies outside the scope of this book and would require the use of information derived from my personal experience as a diplomat, on which, as explained in the Preface, I am unable to draw. I believe the record contains much more of success than failure. But I also believe that if the weaknesses I detect in the present policy-making process were corrected, the potential for successful international activity in the future would be significantly increased. I turn now to the problems which, in my view, handicap the process and to possible solutions.

6

PROBLEMS AND SOLUTIONS

'Civil servants find problems for every solution.' When a young diplomat I heard this comment from the late Lord Caradon who, as a Labour government minister, headed the United Kingdom mission to the United Nations from 1964 to 1970. I am not sure that civil servants should be exclusively tarred with this brush. From the pub to the Cabinet room the initial effect of any new idea is usually to stir up objections. But in this chapter I take up Lord Caradon's challenge. Given the way the foreign policy-making process works today and the complexity of the international environment, what are the weaknesses and what the remedies?

British foreign policy-making in recent times is not, in my view, predominantly a tale of problems, weakness and failure but one of considerable success, albeit handicapped by the division of political and public opinion over Europe. As a recent practitioner I am prejudiced. But I am strengthened in my view by what I have often heard from practitioners from other countries. So great is the natural courtesy of diplomatic colleagues, and their ability to flatter, that I made a practice (as I believe they did in reverse) of dividing their compliments by half. They may have reservations about the substance of this or that aspect of British policy. But I am sure it is their general view that the British policy-making machine is highly professional and that it usually responds to the daily challenge of international events with exceptional efficiency. Britain's world-wide coverage of situations through its extensive network of overseas missions is seen as a great strength. The quality of its armed forces, the British Council's educational and cultural activity abroad and the role of the BBC are much envied. I have been told, so many times that I have to believe it, that British foreign policy is better co-ordinated than that of most other countries. That is usually very evident at international meetings. It is rare for a British delegate to have to say that the views he or she has expressed represent the position of the Foreign Office but have not yet been endorsed by some other Whitehall department. The British practice is that delegations speak for the government as a whole, not an individual department. Circumstances can arise where an official must state that his position has not yet received ministerial authority but that is comparatively rare. These may seem mundane points but they are of great practical importance in international negotiation. Delegations that reveal that their departments at home are at loggerheads over an issue, or that they are speaking without the proper authority of their government, are in a weak position to negotiate. The British missions to major international organizations such as the European Union, the United Nations and NATO, or our delegations at key international summits such as the G8 gathering, have a reputation for coherent policy and mastery of the subject matter.

One other important strength should be noted. Despite a degree of erosion of the concept of public service, to which I shall return, that ideal is still remarkably strong in the Diplomatic Service at home and abroad. Indeed, when head of that service I regarded it as our strongest asset. It was the essential motivation for officials at home, who often worked abnormally long days under exceptional pressure, and for staff abroad who, contrary to the popular image of the glossiness of diplomatic life, often carried out their work in conditions of discomfort, stress and danger. In a world where the notion of a career for life is outdated and where the practice of moving from organization to organization to obtain greater material benefits is common the concept of working for a country rather than for purely personal goals is less fashionable than it was. But it still brings fulfilment to large numbers of people, young and old.

Objective surveys of the cultural attitudes of the policy-makers are rare. But the image which is sometimes presented of a Foreign Office which is culturally monolithic and typecast in its behaviour and views has always seemed to me wrong or at the very least out of date. As the Foreign Office opens its door more to specially arranged events for the general public, for the ethnic communities and for schoolchildren, the outdated image is at last receding. One recent study may help the process. A 1992 survey based on interviews of nearly two hundred individuals from the 'foreign policy élite' concluded that

> the consistency with which . . . a strong minority view occurs suggests that the probability of the British foreign policy process being seriously affected by the 'group think' phenomenon is relatively low: dissenting voices exist in most issue-areas and the individuals concerned are clearly prepared to express their dissent openly and explicitly.[1]

The problems, to my mind, lie elsewhere. They are partly internal – questions of workload, machinery, resources, culture (though in a different sense to that discussed above) and the link between ministers and officials; and partly external – questions related to the use of outside sources of information and advice and to the issues of public information and debate.

Those who argue that the overloading of ministers and their too frequent rotation have an adverse impact on the policy-making process are, in my view, right. The problem exists throughout Whitehall and is certainly evident in the Foreign Office. Experienced Cabinet ministers who came to the job of Foreign Secretary told me how relatively unburdened their former posts seemed in retrospect. Foreign governments are often bemused by the rapidity with which the junior minister responsible for relations with their particular country changes. Ministerial rotation will always be dependent on political factors, and no neat solution is available. But if concerns about the quality of policy-making in Britain deepen, Prime Ministers may give greater priority to retaining ministers in post for longer than has been the case in recent years.

I suspect that Foreign Secretaries will always be overloaded, however much they try to delegate to junior ministers and however radically they change their working methods. If a spare hour appears in the day's diary, there are always more than enough claimants to fill it. The intensity of unavoidable foreign travel, the frequency with which senior foreign visitors seek meetings in London, the claims of the media on ministerial time, the volume of paperwork that can be done only by the Foreign Secretary, all are unlikely to change substantially. So the issue becomes one of prioritization. If, as I believe, reputations are in the end made or unmade by policy – and it is the soundness of policy which primarily determines how successful Britain is in pursuing its overseas interests – then time and space for policy-thinking have to be found and preserved by whatever bureaucratic device is most effective: regular policy meetings on specific issues attended by key ministers and officials, away-days on larger strategic issues, special attention to policy papers as distinct from the rest of the clutter. But, as I know from experience, it will require an iron will on the part of the Foreign Secretary and his

Private Office to make these things happen. Events will get in the way if they are allowed to.

Prioritization could take another form. Despite all the managerial exhortations over the years to delegate work, both to allow those at the top more time for the big issues and to give more junior staff greater responsibility, the trend in Whitehall has often seemed to be in the opposite direction. Ministers appear to me to be involved in detail to a much greater extent than in earlier times. And not just to me. Andrew Marr believes that it is because ministers 'have lost so much "posh power" (over currencies, trade, defence) that they have been sweeping up for themselves, and their appointees, more down-to-earth or "common" powers over schools, training and so on'.[2] Based on his experience of international organizations, such as the EU, the G8 and the UN, Douglas Hurd writes that 'Heads of governments and ministers are beset by minor proposals that should either be settled at working level or abandoned. There is much frantic discussion of detail, too little leisurely development of personal trust and analysis of fundamentals.'[3] Clearly, if that is the nature of the process, sound policy is at risk.

One reason for this preoccupation with detail is probably the increased expectation of the media – and to some extent Parliament and public opinion – that ministers should be ready, at the drop of a hat, to engage in minute discussion of the latest event. Inquiries into events that have apparently gone wrong also tend to assume that ministers and senior officials should have been on top of every detailed aspect of the affair. The

Scott Inquiry of 1992–6 and the 1998–9 examination of Sierra Leone by the House of Commons Foreign Affairs Committee considered in exhaustive detail the precise actions which ministers and officials took day by day and sometimes hour by hour. Rigorous examination of the executive's actions is a wholly necessary part of the democratic system. But the more those in government are expected to be masters of detail the less time they will have for the policy-thinking which, in the end, is so much more important. It is not easy to see how the process by which detail rises to the top of government can be reversed. Delegation is always easier in theory than in practice. But the essence of the solution is probably for a deliberate effort to be made by the centre to define afresh, in broad terms, the kind of subject matter which ministers and officials, respectively, are to handle in future, and to make that definition public.

The general problem of overload affects officials as well as ministers. It is a matter of fact, though it is not well recognized publicly, that many Foreign Office officials work unduly long hours and are under considerable and constant pressure. As Permanent Under-Secretary, I expected to be heavily burdened and make no complaint that I was. On five days a week I left home at 7.15 a.m., read the daily newspapers on the way to the office, and worked through the day until, on nights when there was no official entertainment to attend, I reached home, usually with papers to be read there, at around 8 p.m. On a good weekend, I could complete my paperwork during the course of Saturday. But I often worked through the weekend. Many other officials would tell a similar story.

The problem extends well down the chain. In February 1999 there was much publicity for the report of the House of Commons Foreign Affairs Committee on its inquiry into the Foreign Office's handling of events in Sierra Leone, in particular the question of the supply of arms to that country.[4] I saw no publicity for an important section of this report which noted that the resources of the Foreign Office were under considerable strain and stated that 'mistakes and misjudgements are the inevitable result of requiring officials and ministers to work "at or beyond the limits of their capacity"'. The Committee found that the main officials concerned with Sierra Leone were working very long hours, one as much as a seventy-hour week. It described this as unacceptable. The Committee believed that there was something fundamentally wrong with Foreign Office management if officials were regularly expected to work excessive hours. There may be something in this but in my view the primary explanation lies in the lack of adequate resources. If you do not have sufficient people to do the job, those whose responsibility it is will either do the work inadequately or will work excessively long hours in trying to do it adequately, with the risk of mistakes being made.

The Foreign Affairs Committee also considered that part of the problem might lie in the unduly hierarchical nature of the Foreign Office organization, that the need for each person in the hierarchical chain to consider advice on its way to ministers was cumbersome and work-creating rather than work-reducing. As explained in Chapter 4 the hierarchy is a formal structure, but it is by no means rigid. The picture often conjured up of one bureaucrat laboriously passing advice to his immediate senior and the procedure being repeated up the chain until a minister is reached is misleading. Links are bypassed; oral communication replaces written; the whole hierarchical process is often avoided by a single meeting of those concerned.

But the hierarchical structure does have its rationale. It is that each person at a higher link in the chain should, by dint of depth and breadth of experience, be able to bring to a problem greater perspective and insight. In the upper echelons there should be people who have the time to consider broad policy issues related to the medium as well as the short term. To any management consultant seeking savings in expenditure these officials are natural targets since their role may be less precisely defined and apparently less closely geared to practical action than that of more junior officials. But if the capacity to make good policy is to be preserved it makes little sense to reduce the numbers of those best equipped by experience and proven talent to provide sound policy advice. For these reasons I sought to preserve the senior structure of officials and more or less succeeded. It will no doubt be questioned again.

But there *are* changes that could be made that would free up more time for careful policy-making. I give but one example which is close to home. John Dickie, a journalist who knows the Foreign Office better than most, advocates freeing the Permanent Under-Secretary 'from the managerial functions which have been loaded on to him in recent times . . . he should be the politico-economic supremo always on hand to advise the Foreign Secretary without being distracted by management investigations', his administrative functions being trans-ferred to an 'executive director responsible for ensuring a cost-efficient service'.[5] I have much sympathy with this and believe that if priority for policy-making is to be effectively reasserted, changes of this kind will be required. More than one Cabinet minister has told me in the past that what he wanted above all from his Permanent Secretary was policy advice but that what he invariably found was that the incumbent was preoccu-pied with management and administration. The proposal is more radical than it may seem. It would mean that the Permanent Secretary would no longer be the Accounting Officer for his department: another designated officer would be responsible to central government and to Parliament for the proper expenditure of public funds. Yet it is from that responsibility that most of the Permanent Secretary's management functions flow. I can well imagine that the Parliamentary Public Accounts Committee would be reluctant to abandon the practice of summoning the official Head of the Department to explain why financial matters have apparently gone wrong. But this has to be balanced against the improve-ments in policy formulation which would, I believe, result. A specially designated alternative senior official should be a perfectly adequate substitute. The Permanent Secretary is only the most conspicuous example of an official whose management responsibilities limit time for policy-making. Ways of reprioritizing policy-making need to be sought throughout the hierarchy.

Another cause of overload, especially at the top, is the growth of summitry and international conferences in general. It seems to be an iron law of international diplomacy that once a particular form of summit has been institutionalized it can never be abandoned. Most international conferences, whatever else they may disagree about, can usually be relied upon to vote for another, on the same subject, to be held in the not so distant future. The European Council, which brings together heads of government of EU member-states at least three times a year, is an indispensable part of the EU decision-making machinery. Yet though its working methods, and the subject-matter brought before it, often leave much to be desired, it is here to stay. Commonwealth summits have been somewhat shortened in length in recent years but it is still questionable whether the importance of the business transacted justifies the time spent by heads of government. I am also doubtful whether all the effort and expense of G8 summits are justified by the results, especially now that so much of their time is devoted to communiqués and other media requirements. Time and again those who attend say that next year's must be different – less media, fewer outward trappings, a better-focused agenda and greater informality. But the host government for the next event usually finds that on the whole it is not possible to change things much. I am not hopeful that summitry will be substantially reduced though, objectively, I think it could be achieved without much loss. Many governments would welcome a reduction of the burden but to propose this would, admittedly, be a matter of some political delicacy.

Overload apart, what of the effectiveness of the policy-making machinery? As stated earlier, I see little fundamentally wrong with the day-to-day conduct of foreign policy, the decision-taking related to events as they occur. It is in this area – where the bulk of foreign policy is made – that the machine functions at its best. But longer-term planning is another matter. It is not a question, as some critics suggest, of Foreign Office officials being averse to planning (except in the sense that we all tend to be when we are busy with something else). On the contrary, it has long been the practice to put some of the ablest officials at the head of, or in, the Policy Planning Staff. In recent memory former heads have become Ambassadors in France, Germany and Russia, High Commissioner in India, and Political Director, all very senior appointments. I have described already how the planning apparatus worked in formal terms when I supervised it (see pp. 87–8). The problem lies in the interchange between officials and ministers. In my experience Foreign Secretaries have usually found it difficult to make adequate time for substantial papers relating to the medium term when there are so many issues of more immediate concern to handle. This is understandable. But policy-planning without ministerial involvement and endorsement risks becoming almost entirely academic. The planners themselves need the sense that ministers are interested in their product if it is to be of high quality.

There is a risk in any organization that planning work will be relegated to the sidelines as being too speculative, too unrealistic to affect the serious business of decision-taking. The point of planning is not, however, to predict the future. Anyone who considers that to be a useful foreign policy-making function might ponder two quotations:

In European diplomacy 'the sky has never been more perfectly blue'.

So stated Lloyd George in July 1914 shortly before the outbreak of the First World War.[6] And,

There will still be two Germanys fifty years from now.

That statement was made by Professor D. Cameron Watt in September 1989 shortly before German reunification.[7]

The purpose is not to predict confidently what will happen in the world, a task for which there is little science, but by concentrating minds on alternative scenarios and possible developments, to make today's decisions sounder and more likely to stand the test of events. More thought needs to be given to the methodology that might be used in arriving at the best possible analysis of likely developments. Not much guidance was available to Foreign Office planners during my time in office (and I must take responsibility for that). They knew that part of their task was to think and write about future scenarios but the method was left to their intelligence. In the annual Roskill Lecture at Churchill College, Cambridge, on 16 February 1999, Sir Colin McColl, Head of MI6 from 1988 to 1994, addressed the question of 'Risks and Forecasts in World Affairs'. Commenting on the run on the Thai currency in June 1997 and subsequent economic shocks in Indonesia, Malaysia and Russia, he stated: 'What was surprising and disquieting, not only to observers but to the practitioners of finance, was the fact that, in an age of unparalleled sophistication, none of the major players had been able to forecast that a crisis of major proportions was on the way.'

In his view there was a weakness in our armour, namely that we had no formal method of measuring risks which lie just over the horizon, say in the next five years. He offered such a methodology based on four ground rules. First, no commitment should be made to a specific outcome since that is to confuse the forecasting of likelihood with that of fact (and is likely to discredit the risk-assessment machinery). Second, read and digest all relevant scenarios and use them as background for worrying and hoping, thereby concentrating minds on future possibilities. Third, ask the questions which really matter, thinking in particular of the most and least welcome outcomes. Fourth, concentrate on the concept of *likelihood* rather than risk or threat. Using those ground rules, address the question under consideration in terms of the likelihood of a specific outcome. For example, what is the likelihood of a Chinese currency devaluation? Identify the main factors which are driving towards that outcome, the main factors which are impeding it, and the secondary factors capable of strengthening or weakening the main factors. The key step is then to make a judgement of the likelihood of the specified outcome based upon the balance of these various forces. The final task is thereafter to watch like a hawk for changes which could affect any one of the various factors and so alter the existing balance.

I suspect that many involved in planning and risk assessment in government would feel that their work had unconsciously used some part or other of this methodology. But I also suspect that its conscious and deliberate use would improve the present capacity for forecasting and risk assessment.

There will still be a problem of ministerial digestion. The product of each planning exercise needs to be sufficiently crisp, realistic and relevant to engage busy political minds. The chances of success might be better if, instead of producing a series of planning papers throughout the year, a body of planning assumptions and recommendations were presented to ministers, say, twice a year at the strategy sessions suggested above. But then those sessions would have to happen. Otherwise planning work would virtually disappear.

Weakness in planning is probably a Whitehall-wide phenomenon. In a speech in December 1998, the Permanent Secretary of the Department for Education and Employment stated that 'Modernising policy requires a much greater emphasis being placed on contingency planning and risk assessment . . . Sometimes policy has been developed with just one future scenario in mind.' I completed this book before the outcome of the BSE enquiry was known. But according to press reports, Keith Meldrum, the government's former chief veterinary officer, told the inquiry that 'there had never been a contingency plan prior to 1996 should a link be discovered between BSE and the new strain of CJD' (that is, between the animal disease and the human disease).[8] Later, William Waldegrave, a former Minister of Agriculture, explained that contingency planning had not been carried out 'because it would in effect have meant planning for the failure of the government's policy on BSE and would have taken too much time and manpower'.[9] It is arguable that from the time a link between BSE and CJD became hypothetically possible, planning to prepare for such an ominous development should have been instituted. It is easy to understand how contingency planning is sidelined in a busy department which is preoccupied with the urgency of the daily agenda. But such planning is important enough to justify entrenchment in the Whitehall culture so that time and resources *are* found for it.

The question of resources for policy work more generally cannot be avoided. In my career as a diplomat priorities have varied, as they will tend to. There were periods when commercial work – export and investment promotion – was determined to be the first concern. At other times it was thought (briefly) that the government should no more intervene in this area than in any other private sector activity. Security issues have had their innings as the major concern, as have information work and 'presentation'. There have been repeated attempts to downplay the importance of political work, the business of collecting and analysing information about overseas countries and issues, and incorporating the results in policy advice to ministers. Neither the Duncan Report nor the Berrill Report discussed in an earlier chapter treated this as an area of the highest priority, but instead argued for its reduction. I am unrepentant in believing that political work, as I have defined it, is the essential foundation of foreign policy-making. In practice, it is political and security issues which take up most of a Foreign Secretary's time. Even as the international agenda enlarges to embrace trans-frontier issues such as migration and international crime, it is the political and security aspects of these which are likely to dominate policy-thinking. From a still wider point of view, if Britain is to continue to play an effective role as a permanent member of the UN Security Council and a member of other international organizations, it needs its own high-quality political information about the situations and issues which come before these bodies.

There is a sense in which political work underlies practically all of the Foreign Office's activity. I have no doubt that support for British business overseas should be a primary task. I devoted much time to this myself. Some British firms, typically the small and medium-sized ones, want straightforward commercial assistance – for example a report on a particular market sector, the location of a commercial agent or help with a trade fair. But I increasingly found that senior British businessmen wanted, first and foremost, a political account of the country in which they were proposing to sell or invest, an assessment of its likely stability, of how and by whom decisions in that country were taken. Many went to great pains to secure and study that assessment before they took sizeable expenditure decisions. They did not often need Foreign Office advice on how to sell their product. That was their expertise, not ours.

Then, a large number of British citizens live overseas. Much larger numbers travel abroad each year. Arithmetic suggests that there will, unfortunately, be more rather than fewer cases of British expatriate communities being urgently evacuated from a country in a dangerous condition and perhaps more British nationals caught up in terrorist incidents (and certainly more requiring the more conventional kinds of consular assistance when they are abroad and travel advice before holidays and other overseas visits). The handling of these often very difficult situations again depends on how accurately the Foreign Office and the overseas posts understand the country and know its decision-makers. Even what is known as 'public diplomacy', the presentation of British policies, aims and achievements to the rest of the world, will be ineffective if it is simply designed at home in ignorance of the target audience.

Much thought has been given in recent years to the

projection of the British image abroad. This is a major Foreign Office function, pursued through its information services and its programmes for bringing overseas visitors and scholars to Britain and through the British Council and the BBC World Service. The activities of the Council and the World Service in this area are relatively well known, those of the Foreign Office less so. In 1996/7 the Foreign Office supplied almost a million publications to its overseas missions for distribution overseas. The first Foreign Office interactive CD-Rom, on the environment, was launched. The 'FCO-on-line-website' was being increasingly used, 25,000 documents being downloaded each week. Some eighty hours of television programmes and more than two hundred hours of radio, in eight languages, were produced for overseas use. About a hundred and seventy foreign TV stations were drawing on the Foreign Office-funded daily satellite TV news service. Many specific projects were devised and implemented to convey an image of contemporary Britain to overseas audiences. In April 1998, the Foreign Secretary established 'FCO Panel 2000', with private sector representation, to produce a strategy for the presentation of Britain world-wide.

Government activity of this kind can do only so much to fashion the image of Britain in the world. The larger part of that image is determined by the way in which the world's media cover British events, achievements and failures, by the impressions made on the millions of tourists and other visitors to Britain and by other flows of information. Government activity is much less likely to influence mass audiences than key opinion-makers in foreign countries, at whom it is primarily directed. Nevertheless, I think the case for such effort by government is strong, both because there is a need to counteract the stock images of Britain which the media tend to convey and which are often outdated, and because government activity can be more precisely targeted. But this whole effort to present Britain abroad needs to be based on careful political analysis of the countries concerned.

One significant component of the British image abroad is often overlooked, namely the network of British diplomatic posts. In major world capitals, including London, embassies and other diplomatic missions are usually a relatively small element in the life of the city or country concerned. But in most capitals they loom larger. They may well occupy some of the most prestigious buildings in town. Their activities are frequently prominently reported by the local media. They are much visited by businessmen, visa applicants and others. And they are a base for important cultural, commercial and other promotional activity. Every well-run British embassy is a place where key political and other personalities from the country concerned come to be entertained and to talk. Part of their impression of Britain is formed by the style of the building, its occupants and their activities. It is therefore desirable that the British embassy conveys an accurate and representative image of the country. I wish it always did.

In a relatively small number of capitals Britain possesses

embassy buildings which are grand in scale and of historical and architectural interest. Where these are properly used (as I think most, if not all, of them are) to present modern Britain in its best manifestations they are invaluable instruments of British influence. It is prestigious buildings, such as those in Paris, Washington and Rome, which come to mind when most people see or hear a reference to a British embassy, largely because of stock media images of the alleged 'champagne lifestyle' of British diplomats. But they are far from being the norm. In addition to the grand embassies, there are a range of smaller, modern buildings well-adapted to their purpose. But there are also an unfortunately large number which by their appearance, design and location convey an impression of Britain that is hardly worthy of the country's standing and achievements and that do not provide adequate facilities for modern diplomacy and overseas representation.

It is all a question of money, of course, but it seems not unreasonable that embassies, whose very function is to represent Britain's reputation and interests overseas, should be places which are modern, efficient, safe and comfortable for occupants and foreign visitors alike, and of which British visitors can be reasonably proud. Too commonly this is not so. Nor is all this irrelevant to the policy-making process. As I emphasize separately, good policy decisions in London are closely dependent on the flow of sound information from overseas missions. The capacity to collect and analyse that information can be much constrained if working conditions are inadequate or if the British embassy is not a place which opinion-formers are keen to visit.

Good policy-making cannot take place in a vacuum. Policy decisions based on inadequate information and assessment may turn out to be anything from unfortunate to calamitous. The judgement as to whether at any one time sufficient resources are being devoted to political work is difficult. But my considered view is that the unremitting pressure on budgets over many years has created a situation where fewer resources are allocated to this activity than should be. Geographical departments in the Foreign Office, which often handle situations of considerable significance for British interests, such as the Gulf War, the Arab-Israeli dispute and Bosnia, are very much smaller than they were twenty years ago and command much less genuine regional expertise. Overseas missions in general spend much less time on political analysis than they formerly did and in many cases are so small that they have at best very limited capability for this work. I am sure that detailed case studies would justify these assertions.

Take the case of Albania in early 1997 when a corrupt pyramid-selling scheme collapsed, aggrieved Albanians took to the streets, public order disintegrated and the British community had to be evacuated quickly. Judgements in London had to be taken on the basis of political analysis supplied, initially, by two diplomats in Tirana, then the total complement of the British embassy in that country. It is no criticism of them to say that with all the other tasks on which they were necessarily engaged in the period before the crisis they were hardly likely to have acquired the deep knowledge of the country and its main personalities which is so crucial in a crisis of this sort.

Another case is Central Asia, when, with the break-up of the Soviet Union, that area emerged into the daylight. Very little knowledge of the new states was available in London. Central Asia quickly became of great interest to British companies, particularly those working in the energy and mineral fields. There was a growing demand for well-informed British missions, able to advise companies on political and other factors which would affect their investments. But adequate resources were not available. The British missions in the Central Asian states are still very small compared with those of our commercial competitors, and British firms remain concerned about this. In the case of foreign policy-making, policy-thinking (as distinct from medium-term planning) cannot be farmed out to a special unit. It has to be part and parcel of the work of most Foreign Office departments and most overseas missions. It needs people and time.

British diplomacy is sometimes criticized, and perhaps with some justification, for being unduly defensive, too risk-averse. Put another way, there is often a demand for 'initiative diplomacy'. With our inherited and extensive experience of the world and of diplomatic action, and given our professional assets, there is a good case for more activity of that sort, always provided that it is designed to promote an identifiable and worthwhile British objective. But initiatives cannot begin and end with a ministerial speech or some other kind of 'launch'. A serious proposal, perhaps to negotiate an end to a conflict or a dispute between two states that want that service, is likely to require a dedicated effort by a team of diplomatic experts over months if not years. They would be hard to come by in present circumstances where resources are fully stretched in the handling of more routine diplomacy. In 1996, when the government decided to make a new effort to solve the problem of the divided island of Cyprus, it appointed a retired diplomat, Sir David Hannay, to conduct the effort. It was sensible to use his outstanding abilities but his appointment also demonstrated the limited ability of the Foreign Office to conduct initiative diplomacy by using its serving personnel.

Similar points arise with the Common Foreign and Security Policy of the European Union. As seen above, the CFSP is an important dimension of British foreign policy. But its success in terms of substantially influencing international events has so far been very limited. It has been largely declaratory in nature. Agreement on public statements of a common position has been relatively easy to achieve. Meaningful common action in the form of sustained and serious diplomacy has been much more elusive. This is partly because the declaratory statements are not backed by a capacity for power-projection but also partly because the capacity for political analysis is weak. A former diplomat with substantial EU experience has argued the case for the establishment of a CFSP Analysis Unit to provide the Union with a collective fact-finding, analytical and policy capacity. But he believes that this and other institutional improvements will work effectively only if the CFSP is able to harness the experience and influence contributed by individual member-states with a strong foreign policy background and a global reach, in particular France, Germany and the United Kingdom. Moreover, he considers that the world-wide network of diplomatic missions of the member-states will need to be more effectively and systematically placed at the service of the CFSP machinery.[10] Jacques Delors, former President of the Commission, draws the lesson from Bosnia that a planning and analysis capacity is necessary at the European level, perhaps modelled on the lines of the US National Security Council.[11] Unless and until a European foreign policy replaces the national foreign policies of member-states − in my view at best a very distant prospect − the effectiveness of the CFSP will depend heavily on the policy capacity of national foreign offices and their diplomatic missions. If that is weak − and I fear it is weaker than it should be − the common policy machinery will be severely hampered.

It is sometimes suggested that the role of providing information about overseas activity can nowadays safely be left to the media. I am sure that is not so. Certainly, the media will usually be the first to report events, though the need to meet tight deadlines and deliver 'newsworthy' stories may distort the reporting. But the government machine needs a different kind of information, for example a confidential account from a Prime Minister of how a situation has arisen and what he plans to do about it. A trusted British diplomat will normally be able to obtain that information and, with his or her knowledge of the speaker and the country, give an assessment of its value. The same Prime Minister will tell journalists only what he wishes to be publicly reported.

The media's coverage of the world is very patchy. Crises, of whatever kind, will of course attract their attention. Some countries are regarded as important enough to warrant regular coverage. But the large majority of countries escape the attention of the media for weeks and months at a time. When I was Ambassador to Jordan from 1984 to 1988 it required a striking development in the Arab-Israeli situation or a spectacular terrorist incident or a visit by the British Prime Minister to get Jordan into the pages of a British newspaper. But government required regular reports and analyses of Jordan's thinking on the peace process, on its economic development and its political stability to enable policy judgements to be made. The confidential access which I, like others who filled the post, had to the late King Hussein, members of the royal family, the government and other Jordanians enabled me and my staff to provide London with the advice and information it needed. Anyone who relied on the media for an understanding of Jordan would have been poorly supplied. That example could be replicated in scores of countries across the world.

Those who are prepared to depend on the media for information about events perhaps need to consider what is happening to the production of 'news' in the modern world. Richard Reeves, an American journalist, has commented that the world of the new generation of television-makers 'looked like news, but after a while you realized that it was actually a new mix of entertainment elements – celebrities, blood, fire, sports, sex, mixed with stories to make you feel good about yourself and bad about your government'. He quotes another American journalist as admitting that 'if readers said they wanted more comics and less foreign news, in a market-driven economy, I'm going to give them more comics and less foreign news'. Yet another is reported as saying that his company was '"breaking the mold" and would cut back on "dull" stories from Washington and foreign countries'. US national television coverage of foreign stories, measured in minutes, dropped by almost two-thirds in just four years, from 1992 to 1996.[12] Britain has not gone as far as America – yet. But as news increasingly becomes entertainment, governments will need to rely ever more on their own sources of information and analysis.

So it is my contention that political work is fundamental to the formulation of foreign policy because the key issues are of a political nature and because support for British industry in its overseas activities, advice and assistance to British citizens abroad, the presentation of the country's image to overseas audiences and the British contribution to the CFSP all depend on a sound capacity for political analysis. That capacity is, in my view, not as strong as it once was or as it now needs to be.

My last point on the internal workings of the policy process relates to the role of Cabinet. To remedy the perceived decline in strategic discussion and decision-taking in Cabinet various proposals have been advanced, for example for the creation of an inner cabinet[13] or a Cabinet Strategic Planning Committee.[14] Institutional change of this kind is unlikely to happen because of foreign policy considerations. The role of Cabinet will be what the Prime Minister of the day, and his or her colleagues, want it to be. That is unlikely to extend to regular discussion of foreign policy issues. But in principle it seems desirable that there should be some provision for high-level strategic discussion of Britain's overseas interests and role, especially as the cross-border issues discussed elsewhere in this book become increasingly salient. Despite the uneven historical experience of Chequers-type seminars, occasional meetings of this kind bringing together key ministers involved in international issues under the Prime Minister's chairmanship would probably give more strategic direction to overseas activities.

Foreign policy-making in the future is likely to become more open, to involve more external actors and, perhaps, though this is less predictable, to stimulate more public debate. We have already come some distance. I have described earlier the existing links between the Foreign Office and business representatives, non-governmental organizations and academic and other experts (see pp. 97–100). The present government has notably incorporated external experts in important policy-making exercises such as the Defence Review of 1997/8. The Foreign Secretary's new Mission Statement of May 1997 opened up a valuable debate with non-governmental organizations, for example at a One World Action seminar (see p. 101). The relevance of such developments is two-fold. Ideas from within government can be tested against external views and use can be made of the many valuable sources of information and expertise on foreign policy issues that exist outside the government machine. One example will suffice to demonstrate the general proposition: non-governmental organizations and aid agencies working in the Sudan, especially in the south, are, because of the circumstances in that benighted country, likely to have more knowledge of the situation on the ground than a small embassy in Khartoum can acquire by its own efforts.

The task is to harness external advice of this and other kinds. The problem is to find the time and effective procedures for doing so. With the best will in the world, ministers and officials often find it difficult to make space in the average working day for the careful and detailed consultation with the many interest groups available which is ideally required. But it should be done, by whatever bureaucratic methods can be devised, because the days have gone when it is sensible to rely on a monopoly of knowledge and advice within the official machine. In the speech quoted on pp. 140–1 the Permanent Secretary of the Department for Education and Employment argued that 'Creative organizations shamelessly use other people's thinking wherever possible' and that good policy demands that 'wherever possible we involve interests outside Whitehall'. I agree. The process of engaging outside advice should not, however, disturb the role of officials as the primary source of advice to ministers since they alone have the constitutional responsibility and the necessary impartiality to carry out that function. But there is no reason why it should.

Involving outside organizations in policy formulation is not a problem-free process. Some governments are being pro-active in involving the public. Consultation is being developed to identify problems and issues, to obtain views on policy choices and to seek reactions to existing policies and programmes. Focus groups, special surveys and complaint mechanisms are being used to test and improve public service. While many of these techniques are useful they make the policy process more complex, more time-consuming and more expensive. They need skills which may not be readily available inside the government machine and place strains on already overloaded capacity.

Then, the active involvement of interest groups may make the policy process less controllable. Some groups will employ tactics such as judicial challenge and disruptive public protest. There is a danger of interest groups capturing public policy and overshadowing the views of the silent majority or the overall public interest. It is right, therefore, that, as noted in a recent OECD study (from which many of these points are taken), governments should approach interest groups with healthy scepticism.[15] Nevertheless, governments can no longer expect to make policy without a good deal of public involvement, and the benefits of seeking outside advice and information are likely to outweigh the disadvantages.

The image of the Foreign Office as a closed shop whose policy-making is entirely immune from public inspection should have been interred once and for all in March 1995 when literally hundreds of experts with an interest in foreign affairs were invited to a public conference, organized by the Royal Institute of International Affairs in association with the government, and were encouraged to participate in a day-long debate on all aspects of British foreign policy.[16] The event attracted a good deal of media and other comment at the time and stimulated longer-term reflections on Britain's overseas role.[17] Resources will not allow the staging of major events of this kind very frequently. But there is everything to be said for encouraging wider and more informed debate on British foreign policy. There is no shortage of published material. The Foreign Office's 1998 Annual Report to Parliament lists 42 keynote speeches by ministers and a selective list of 100 official and other publications relating to foreign policy, all produced in the previous twelve months.[18] But much of the material, though available, is unlikely to be widely read. A more focused statement leading to broader debate seems to me desirable. I believe it would be worth implementing the old idea of an annual White Paper on foreign policy, leading to an annual debate in Parliament. I noted earlier the anomaly whereby the Ministry of Defence produces such a document but the Foreign Office does not. The case for an annual foreign policy document of this kind is in my view strengthened by the

ever-increasing involvement of many Whitehall departments in international issues, the cross-curricular nature
of many of those issues and the consequent need for a
well co-ordinated, regular explanation of the government's overseas policy.

Even if all the above proposals for improving the policy
process are implemented they will have limited impact on
the quality of policy unless two fundamental requirements are met: a strong working relationship between
ministers and officials on policy issues, and a clear and
sustained message from the centre of government that
policy formulation is not *a* but, I would argue, *the* priority task.

I approach the first issue as a strong believer in the
crucial value of genuine dialogue between ministers and
officials in policy-making and in the classic formula that
officials advise and ministers decide. The Civil Service
Code states:

> The constitutional and practical role of the Civil Service is,
> with integrity, honesty, impartiality, and objectivity, to assist
> the duly constituted government, of whatever political
> complexion, in formulating policies of the government,
> carrying out decisions of the government and administer-
> ing services for which the government is responsible.[19]

And the former 'Questions of Procedure for Ministers',
now called the Ministerial Code, which is issued by every
Prime Minister when a new government takes office and
which is now a public document, lays on ministers 'the

duty to give fair consideration and due weight to informed and impartial advice from Civil Servants, as well as to other considerations and advice, in reaching decisions'.[20]

Concern has been expressed by outside observers about the apparent erosion of these precepts under various pressures (see Chapter 1). There is a fairly widespread impression that at times in the last decade or two ministers have been inclined to regard civil servants not as policy advisers but merely as implementers of policies separately decided by ministers, as managers rather than policy-thinkers. Advice from political and external sources has been preferred to that offered by the official machine. The quality of advice provided by civil servants has sometimes been regarded as unimaginative, defensive and, worse, based on a desire to protect or advance separate departmental policies springing not from ministerial decision but from the personal conviction of the civil service or groups within it. In turn, civil servants are believed to feel that their advice is not sought or valued, that ministers are less inclined than they were to debate policy advice rationally with their officials, that good policy-making is no longer regarded as a ministerial priority, and that the very concept of public service has been denigrated.

At any given time general assertions as to the behaviour of ninety or so ministers and thousands of civil servants are likely to be pretty misleading. The relationship will always have its ups and downs; and when it is down there are always plenty of ministers and officials who regret the fact and want to see it restored. My personal experience has been that the best policy decisions have come from a process in which advice is given frankly by officials, is challenged and discussed by ministers and is measured against advice from other sources. That is how the process has often worked. I think there *is* justification for some of the criticism that has been made of officials in the past, that advice was at times unimaginative and attitudes were too defensive. I am quite clear in my own mind that any disposition by officials to embrace causes or positions that do not conform with ministerial policy is wholly to be deplored. It distorts the policy-making process in a democratic system and quickly leads to a breakdown of trust. That said, I detect a need to reassert the role of officials in policy-making, to make plain that they are looked to as the primary source of advice, but equally that they are expected to be open to ideas from all sources, inside and outside government, and to channel the best possible advice to ministers regardless of its source. More attention will need to be paid to training officials in that role. Each government department would do well to ensure that it has the policy skills and experience to be and remain the government's preferred source of policy advice. Much specialized training is given to civil servants nowadays. In the Foreign Office many of us spent time at the London Business School on management courses. There is extensive training on commercial work, on information skills and much else. But there is little training on policy-making.

As this book was being completed new legislation on freedom of information was under discussion. In due course this will doubtless result in a further opening up of the policy-making system to public scrutiny. I favour that in general, but I hope it can be achieved without impairing the confidentiality of official advice to ministers. Frank advice on delicate subjects cannot be expected if officials feel it will shortly be in the public domain.

In general, official advisers need to receive from the centre of government a clear message that policy-making is regarded as the essential function of government, on the basis of which good implementation, presentation and management can proceed but for which they can be no substitute. We need a culture which elevates policy-making to its proper place and that banishes the disparaging term 'policy wonks' entirely from the lexicon.

I find recent moves in this direction encouraging. In a speech delivered in October 1998 the Prime Minister stated that the government valued public service, that it was not just a job but a vocation, and that the country relied on that ethic of service. He wished to revalue public service and rekindle the enthusiasm that made people become public servants in the first place. But, he continued, many parts of the civil service were still too hierarchical and inward-looking, too short-termist and too risk-averse. A longer-term approach to decision-making was needed, from ministers as well as civil servants. And so were more innovation, more testing of policy by pilot projects, more working across boundaries, more project teams, less hierarchy. The new Centre for Management and Policy Studies, he hoped, would open government up to new thinking from the wider world;[21] and the new Performance and Innovation Unit would help tackle cross-cutting problems;[22] but most new thinking would still take place in the departments of government. We needed to ask ourselves searching questions about policy. Did we devote enough time to developing new policies? Did we know enough about how other countries were tackling the same problems? Did we think sufficiently long-term, sufficiently strategically? Did ministers always act in such a way as to get the best out of the civil service machine? Mr Blair looked forward to seeing the debate develop.[23]

I began my research on this book and developed the main ideas in it before this statement. I hope the product will be of some value in answering these questions and stimulating discussion.

7

AUSTRALIAN INTERLUDE

Policy-making can benefit from the experience of other countries and governments. If that experience is studied carefully and imported with a sensitive awareness of the different circumstances of the originating country, mistakes can be avoided and successes emulated. The policies of others can to a certain extent be used as pilot projects for our own. How far this route can be followed depends on the time and resources available, but it may well be cost-effective. I have long thought that more use could be made of British overseas missions in bringing to London's attention foreign examples of new policy developments across the whole spectrum of government which might be relevant to the thinking of policy-makers in Westminster and Whitehall. And, of course, a certain amount of this is done.

I cautioned in Chapter 2 that there are limits to the

extent to which the British process of making foreign policy can usefully be compared with foreign examples. Some apparently obvious comparators, for example France, Germany and the United States, have governmental systems and foreign policy processes which differ so substantially from our own that their experience cannot easily be transplanted. That should not prevent British policy-makers from drawing such lessons as they can from these countries but there are others where the practice may be more directly beneficial.

In this chapter I consider briefly the case of Australia. Its federal system of government may at first sight make it an odd choice. But as devolution proceeds in Britain that may be less of an obstacle. In any case Australia does otherwise have similar bureaucratic structures to our own and a similar governmental system, and it shares many foreign policy goals with Britain. It is also a country which I was able to study at close quarters in my time there as British High Commissioner (1988–91).

It is the policy-making process which is of most interest here. But I first set the scene. In the last couple of decades Australia has been engaged in redefining its position and role in the world. For many years following the Second World War it still saw its close links with the United States and Western Europe as the essential basis of its international action primarily because Australia's security was regarded, in the last resort, as dependent on America, and because Australian traditions and culture were still closely enmeshed with those of the European countries, especially Britain, to which the large majority of Australians traced their roots. As the links with Western countries weakened, a process given considerable impetus by Britain's entry into the European Community, and as the importance of Australia's economic links with the Asia-Pacific region grew and its intake of immigrants from Asia gradually increased, a process of redefining not just foreign policy goals but the nature of Australian society began. The process is not over. It has stimulated much public debate and it has created strains and tensions. But most Australians and most foreign observers probably regard the transformation as broadly successful.

Given Australia's geographical position in the South Pacific, and the clear desire of the Australian people to form and express a national identity independent of their formerly 'British' identity, a new definition of the country's national interests and international role became inevitable. But the main driving force was economic. Rich in mineral, energy and agricultural resources, Australia had an overwhelming need to develop profitable and reliable markets for its commodities. As the populations of the Asian countries grew and their economies expanded it became clear that the main objective must be to develop the markets which they provided. To achieve this, Australians had to become more aware of, and more knowledgeable about, Asian societies and develop closer political links with their governments, establishing Australia in their eyes as a country with a credible role in the Asia-Pacific region, with things to offer as well as to sell.

In the early 1980s Australian policy-makers saw agricultural exports being increasingly prejudiced by
American and European competition. The idea was conceived of forming a lobby of agricultural exporters to act
as a third force between the United States and the
European Community. In August 1986 a dozen or so
countries were represented at the first meeting of what
became the Cairns Group, whose voice then became an
important element in international negotiation on agricultural trade. In 1987 the former Foreign and Trade
Ministries of the Australian government were amalgamated to form the Department of Foreign Affairs and
Trade with the explicit purpose of giving more prominence to economic and trade issues in Australia's foreign
policy.

Defence policy was also evolving. Following an
impressive study in 1986, a Defence White Paper was
produced in March 1987. This, according to Gareth
Evans, a former Australian foreign minister, was 'the conceptual watershed'. It was 'no longer necessary for
Australia's foreign policy to begin with the assumption
that its first task is to ensure the defence of Australia by
attracting the protective attention of great and powerful
friends'. Instead Australia would depend on 'a coherent
policy of defence self-reliance'.[1] Two years later the same
foreign minister presented to the federal parliament a
statement on Australia's regional security, the main
theme of which was that the country should enhance its
security by 'enmeshing' itself with its immediate and
more distant Asian neighbours through the use of all its

main instruments – diplomacy, defence policy, economic policy, immigration policy and cultural relations.[2]

Substantial foreign policy initiatives followed. There had long been discussion in the Asia-Pacific region about the need to develop and exploit the strengths of the Pacific Rim economies. Early in 1989 the Australian Prime Minister, Bob Hawke, proposed the formation of a group of Asia-Pacific countries to promote more effective economic co-operation in their region and inter-governmental dialogue to advance common interests. An initial meeting was held in Canberra towards the end of that year. Asia-Pacific Economic Co-operation (APEC) was born as a new international organization. In 1989 also, a major report on 'Australia and the Northeast Asian Ascendancy', analysing the country's economic links with that area of key importance to the Australian economy and presenting the arguments for closer Australian engagement, was delivered to the Australian government.[3] These years saw, too, the development of Australian thinking on the situation in Cambodia and an important Australian contribution to the negotiations leading to a peace settlement in that country.

There is an extensive Australian literature on these developments.[4] But the purpose of this brief and superficial summary is simply to provide a backcloth for some observations about how Australian foreign policy was made in the period.

As an observer, close at hand, several points impressed me. First, the intellectual underpinnings of policy-making were strong. The case for Australian

'enmeshment' with the Asia-Pacific region was inten-
sively analysed within the government machine and the
knowledge and expertise of Australia's academic and
other experts effectively harnessed. Second, once the
goal of intensive involvement with Asia had been determined, government policies across the board were
realigned to promote it. For example, the immigration
programme was reoriented to favour Asian immigrants
and a programme introduced in Australian schools
designed to ensure that at least one out of six Asian languages was routinely taught. Third, public debate was
deliberately encouraged by government. The 1989 statement on Australia's regional security referred to above
contained more discussion and analysis of security questions than were common in British public documents of
the period. The Garnaut Report on Australia's relations
with the countries of Northeast Asia was launched by the
then Australian Prime Minister at a press conference
(which I attended) to ensure maximum publicity and
subsequent debate. This was an essential part of the new
policy because the government's aim was nothing less
than to change the mind-set of Australians about their
country's place and role in the world.

We can get closer to the process by which Australian
foreign policy was made. Senator Gareth Evans became
Australia's Minister for Foreign Affairs and Trade in
September 1988. Three months later he delivered a
speech in Canberra on 'Elements in Australian Foreign
Policy-Making'; and some four months after this a
second speech in Melbourne on 'Priorities for Australian

Foreign Policy'. In 1991, still as Foreign Minister, he incorporated this material in a book, *Australia's Foreign Relations in the World of the 1990s*.[5] It is most unusual for any foreign minister to set out, in such detail and so publicly, at the outset of a period in office, an explanation both of how policy is made and of its substance.

On process, Evans explains that the relationship between the Foreign Minister and the Prime Minister was crucial. He and the Prime Minister regularly held brief discussions of foreign policy issues but every few months met for two or three hours or more to work through issues on the foreign policy agenda. The rush of events meant that only a handful of matters would lend themselves to full-scale Cabinet or Cabinet Committee deliberation on the basis of formal papers. Nevertheless, there were sixteen or so such discussions a year. Consultations with other ministers outside the Cabinet framework were more frequent. The policy advice of the Department of Foreign Affairs and Trade was 'crucial'. The policy-makers were also influenced by discussions in the parliamentary Labour Party and its foreign affairs, defence and trade committees (though formal set-piece foreign affairs debates in the federal parliament were fewer than in the past) as well as by formal advisory groups, NGOs and other pressure groups, and academics. As to the media, 'In foreign affairs, however much media interest impacts on ministerial work programmes, it is simply not wise for governments to make policy in response to a media-driven agenda.'[6]

On the substance as distinct from process, Evans argues

that, for all the uncertainties of foreign policy-making, it can and should be an intellectually orderly process. 'There is really no alternative to having a clear-headed appreciation of what one wants to achieve, and what one is likely to achieve, and to allocate more resources of time and energy accordingly.'[7] The concept of national interest is necessarily the starting point in making decisions, though the elements that constitute national interest are not necessarily self-evident. He groups Australia's interests in three categories – geopolitical or strategic, economic and trade, and 'being a good international citizen'. Capacity to influence must be assessed. But effective management of foreign affairs depends not just on being able to recognize opportunities for influence but also on developing and constantly refining priorities, which he then proceeds to define for the benefit of his public audience.

In a final chapter, Evans presents a detailed analysis of Australia's role in the world based on the concept of 'being an effective middle power'. 'The kind of foreign policy Australia has been crafting and implementing in recent years – which might be broadly characterized as middle power diplomacy with an Asian Pacific orientation – has been designed to respond to [the] new internationalist understanding manifestly growing in the Australian community.'[8]

This short summary cannot do justice to the detailed argument of the book. But it is perhaps sufficient to illustrate the conceptual thinking which underlay the substantial shift in Australian foreign policy towards a new degree of engagement with the Asia–Pacific region. This, I should add, was never seen as an exclusive preoccupation by the policy-makers. They envisaged the maintenance of a strong relationship with many other areas of the world. But it became the main objective given Australia's reappraisal of where its economic and security interests lay.

Public debate in Australia is usually vigorous and not exactly punch-pulling, especially where anything emanating from the government in Canberra is concerned. Critics of the extent to which Australia has sought to realign itself with the Asia–Pacific region are easily found and have no doubt been given a new lease of life by the recent problems of some Asian economies. But as an exercise in redefining policy against a clear concept of national interest – an exercise, moreover, conducted openly and with full public debate – this reorientation of foreign policy is of considerable interest to policy-makers elsewhere.

I have discussed earlier the attempt by policy-makers in Britain to devise an overall concept to explain and motivate British foreign policy and have analysed the criticisms made by observers of the apparent failure to do so successfully. In this context it is worth noting one more development in Australian foreign policy-making, the publication in 1997 of the first ever White Paper on Australia's foreign and trade policy.[9] This document considers the forces which, over the next fifteen years, are most likely to influence Australia's external environment and the policy implications which flow from that assessment.

Described as a framework document, it focuses on the conceptual foundations of the government's foreign and trade policy, examining the major challenges for Australia over the period concerned and identifying broad strategies for dealing with them. It does not address resource and operational issues but states that it is clear that Australia will need a high-quality and effective international network if it is to take full advantage of future opportunities.

An advisory panel of distinguished Australians with broad experience in business, government and academia made a major contribution to the document and views were received from representatives of the state and territory governments of Australia as well as business groups and non-governmental organizations. Part of the motivation of the White Paper was that 'Australia must have a Foreign and Trade Policy that the Australian community understands and supports'.

The aim of this policy is described as 'advancing the interests of Australia and Australians'. The basic test to be applied to all actions is that of national interest which 'does not change with a change of government'. Considerable emphasis is placed on bilateral relationships as a means of advancing Australia's interests. These relations are seen as the basic building-block for effective regional and global strategies. Their development would be 'the core part of the government's diplomatic activities'. The approach to multilateral issues would be selective, issues being chosen for their close relevance to national interest. But Australia's interests were global and therefore a foreign and trade policy of broad scope was required.

The two most profound influences on Australia's foreign and trade policy over the next fifteen years would be globalization and the continuing economic rise of East Asia (written of course before the recent downturn in many Asian economies). Strategies for bilateral, regional and multilateral action are elaborated, with particular emphasis on the advancement of security and trade strategies. A central concept is a 'whole-nation' approach which emphasizes the link between domestic policies and foreign and trade policies.

> An integrated framework is crucial to enhancing Australia's international competitiveness. In a global economy the competitiveness of the Australian economy will be the single most important determinant of Australia's future. It is the benchmark against which both domestic and international policy must be measured.

The advancement of Australia's interests is seen as a task 'for all Australians, not just their governments' and one which requires communication and consultation among governments at all levels (that is, federal and state governments), businesses and the community. Policy success would depend on meeting the needs, and reflecting a close understanding of, the interests of all Australians.

Each of these themes is then considered in some detail in a well-produced document of some eighty pages.

The features of the White Paper which relate most clearly to the discussion of policy-making in earlier chapters are: the fact that it was produced at all, for such attempts to elaborate a strategic concept of a country's policy are comparatively rare; that it addressed a fifteen-year perspective; that it was based so firmly on a concept of national interest; that it insisted on the need for the integration of foreign and domestic policy in support of Australia's international aims; and that it placed such emphasis on the need for community support for foreign policy. No doubt the predictions of the continuing economic rise of East Asia look over-optimistic in the light of more recent events but Australia was in good company in not foretelling the later turbulence in Asian economies. Despite this turbulence Australia's dependence on East Asia continues to be substantial.

As British High Commissioner in Australia I attempted to rethink British policy towards the country and base it on what Australia had become rather than what it once was. There was still in Britain at that time a sentimental view of Australia as a piece of Britain in the South Pacific. We had not taken proper account of the strong sense of Australian nationhood. No Australian Prime Minister had paid an official visit to Britain. It was assumed that he would pass through London from time to time, perhaps combining calls on the government with the cricket at Lord's. Stock British images still assumed that the average Australian was white, Anglo-Saxon and lived in the bush though Australian society had long been ethnically diverse and predominantly urban. The reorientation of the country towards Asia was barely appreciated. The rich ethnic mix of Australian society was rarely apparent from the soap operas. And few were aware of the substantial investment by British firms in Australia or of the significant level of two-way trade or the potential it offered as a springboard for exports to and investment in Asia.

With London's help I and my staff set out to modernize British policy towards the country. The key event was a visit by the then Prime Minister, Margaret Thatcher, in 1988. On my advice her several speeches were carefully drafted to demonstrate that Britain fully recognized Australia as an entirely independent state with its own national identity on which Britain had no special claims. The Australian Prime Minister was at last invited to visit London officially, which he did in 1989. Both sides emphasized that they wanted a modern relationship, based in particular on trade and investment in both directions. On her return to London Mrs Thatcher asked her Cabinet ministers to take a new interest in Australia and, in sharp contrast to past years, a considerable number came to see the country for themselves and examine opportunities for increased British activity. The change in approach laid a much healthier basis for dealing with Australia in the future.

When I worked in Canberra I often detected a certain inhibition among Britons and Australians about learning from each other, a reluctance that owes much to outdated views about our respective countries. Hang-ups of that kind are a luxury that cannot easily be afforded now. Where the ideas are good we should seize and exploit them for all they are worth.

8

A CERTAIN IDEA OF BRITAIN

The foreign policy of a state is one element in the sense of identity of its citizens. Recollection of past successes and failures abroad is part of the image which a country has of itself. If the pattern of overseas involvement is one of retreat or defensiveness or failure to achieve what public opinion wants or has been led to want, confidence in the state and feelings of identity with it are weakened. But if it is felt that the country is doing well abroad, maintaining its security, advancing its prosperity, helping to solve international conflicts and problems, bringing relief to suffering, confidence in the state and pride in citizenship are strengthened. Or so I believe.

The professional diplomat's task of representing Britain abroad, promoting its policy, advocating its achievements and explaining and putting in context such failures as there are, is immeasurably easier when there is a good degree of domestic support for both foreign policy itself and domestic developments. As a nation we have been through periods of frustration and disillusionment when little seemed to go right domestically and our capacity to promote our overseas interests was accordingly reduced. The 1970s were, on the whole, such a period. It was then often hard to do more in discussion with foreign governments and others abroad than try to explain that things were not as bad as they were painted. During the 1980s, as domestic reform progressed and Britain became more active and successful in foreign affairs, the task of representation became altogether easier and more pleasant. But even then many engaged in the task, and many other Britons who worked and travelled abroad, were struck by the contrast between the culture of disparagement at home and the altogether more positive light in which serious foreign observers viewed Britain. National institutions from Parliament to the civil service, from the judiciary to the universities, from the police to the health service, attracted a constant barrage of criticism from the media and others. But at the same time they continued to command the admiration of citizens of foreign countries. As economic and other reforms progressed foreign governments dispatched shoals of their own experts to Britain to draw on the experience. It is not that the domestic criticism was always misguided. It was not. But there often seemed to be a lack of perspective in the domestic debate. It was easier to see that failing if you lived and worked abroad and were aware of international comparisons. For so often the comparable institutions in other countries were evidently working much less well, as those who depended on them frequently pointed out.

It is a common experience of British representatives abroad to be told by those with whom they engage not only how admirable many aspects of British society and culture are but how much they want a stronger British interest in their own countries, a more active British involvement in international problems and disputes, a bigger contribution by Britain to promoting the well-being of the world's citizens. Time and again the refrain is heard – in the Middle East, Africa, the Indian subcontinent and elsewhere – that Britain, however controversial its past involvement in a country may have been, understands that country better than anyone else and that such understanding is needed to address today's problems. Even when the rule I have mentioned before is applied – that the compliments of courteous foreigners should be divided by half – the residue is unmistakable: there is often more confidence abroad in Britain's economic strength, domestic resilience, political skills, and diplomatic and military capacity than the ordinary Briton would believe from the television screen or daily newspaper. 'What should they know of England who only England know?' is a question that bears regular pondering.

In the opening words of his *War Memoirs*, de Gaulle spoke of 'a certain idea of France'. All his life, he wrote, he had thought of France in a certain way. The emotional side of him tended to imagine France as dedicated to an exalted and exceptional destiny. Intuitively he felt that Providence had created her either for complete success or for exemplary misfortune. France was not really herself unless she was in the front rank. Only vast enterprises were capable of counterbalancing the ferment of disintegration inherent in her people. France could not be France without greatness. As a young man a certain anxious pride in his country came to him as second nature. Nothing struck him more than the symbols of French glory. Nothing affected him more than the evidence of national successes. Nothing saddened him more profoundly than French weaknesses and mistakes.[1]

De Gaulle's style may not entirely suit the British temperament and any attempt to construct an 'idea of Britain' may only show how elusive that idea is. But it is worth examining some of the recent attempts to describe Britain's status and role in the world. For there is little doubt that a realistic concept which could both inform foreign policy-making and carry conviction with public opinion and inspire its support would be valuable.

There is a varied menu of recent definitions of Britain's status from which to select. The Duncan Report (1968) described Britain as 'a major power of the second order'.[2] Berrill (1977) considered that, though retaining some of the attributes of a great power, Britain was 'on a par with the three other medium-sized countries in the European Community'.[3] A Labour Opposition spokesman opted in 1990 for 'a medium-sized nation on the geographic fringe of Europe'.[4] In a parliamentary debate in 1994 the then Foreign Secretary stated: 'We are a European power with interests that reach far beyond Europe.'[5] The then Leader of the Opposition said in 1995 that our role was to be a

'major global player' but warned that this role would be for-
feited unless we accepted Europe as our base.[6] A previous
practitioner's choice is 'a middling-sized member of Global
United's First Eleven'.[7] An academic expert argues that

> there is simply no convenient classification within which
> Britain fits: it is not a superpower, nor a middle power; it has
> aspects of a great power, but is caught up in a very complex
> set of interdependencies; it has to be involved in bargaining
> within defence and economic alliances and organisations yet
> it is not a small power. No other country has quite this
> profile.[8]

This is more than just playing with words. From a clear
view of Britain's world status, in comparison with that of
other countries, should flow an appreciation of what we
as a country can sensibly seek to do abroad. Britain *is* hard
to classify. It is necessary to take into account the size of its
economy, perhaps ranked fifth in the world or somewhat
lower depending on the criteria used; its membership of
the European Union, the G8 and the United Nations
Security Council; the size and location of its interests
around the globe; the extent to which it can be an autonomous actor; and much else. The definition, if it is to be
of practical use, must eschew nostalgia and inflated notions
based on the past but not succumb to the cynicism with
which the ever-present army of detractors will certainly
bless any formula chosen.

In my view the concept of a 'middle power' will not fit
because that ground is already occupied by Australia and

other similar countries. Britain is clearly to be differentiated from these by its economic weight, spread of interests and prominent position in key international institutions. A satisfactory concept must embrace Britain's membership of, and weight in, the European Union, which is evidently the basis of our future foreign policy. But it must also capture the sense of a country which, for historical and other reasons, has a spread of interests round the globe (not the same as being a global *power*). These bring an involvement in world affairs and opportunities for effective influence which distinguish it from all other European member-states except France. My own choice would be 'a major European power with global interests and responsibilities', the last word deriving primarily but not exclusively from our permanent membership of the UN Security Council and membership of the G8 and our obligations towards our remaining overseas territories.

What role should a country with this kind of status aim to play in the world? There are broadly two ways of approaching this issue. Either one can formulate general principles and then prescribe detailed objectives to implement them. Or one can assess specific British interests and construct general principles on that basis. I prefer the latter since I believe that policy which is not firmly grounded in British interests founders sooner or later in one respect or another and has to be changed. Henry Kissinger writes that the test of the statesman is whether he can discern from the swirl of tactical decisions the true long-term interests of his country and devise an appropriate strategy for achieving them.[9] 'National interest' is a deceptive term and its meaning is often unclear. The concept can be used to construct foreign policy from the bottom up or may simply be invoked to give political justification to a policy already adopted. The vaguer the definition of national interests the harder it is to define practical aims. One commentator has noted the 'deep gap between such vague general values as sovereignty, independence or freedom and any concrete policy objectives'.[10] It is argued that while, in a democracy, voters have a right to a foreign policy that promotes their immediate interests, that notion is too simple to address the real issues which governments – and voters – find before them. So a diverse and complex concept of national interest needs to be developed, as another commentator has explained: 'It includes national security as well as jobs, environmental sustainability as well as trade, the fulfilment of properly chosen humanitarian goals as well as the business interests of British firms.'[11] It has also been argued that the concept, however defined, is too narrow and pursuit of the 'cosmopolitan interest' is recommended instead.[12]

I do not think that the notion of defining national interests is as unworkable as some believe. Nor can I see any other rational means of constructing a policy if it is to endure and be persuasive to an electorate. Unless British voters believe that public expenditure is devoted to causes which relate to their interests they cannot be expected to provide support. But national interests do not need to be narrowly defined. The government of the day can provide its own definition, which can range from the pursuit of purely security and economic objectives to a wider concept embracing humanitarian, environmental and other concerns. That, I believe, must be a political decision. The most interesting part of the discussion about British foreign policy objectives which I held with non-governmental organizations in 1996 (see p. 98) was stimulated by the contention of some of them that the then proclaimed objectives lacked moral purpose. I did not think that true but maintained – as I still would – that it was for political leaders to determine such matters. A public servant must not, of course, promote immoral policy but if each were to bring his or her own set of moral values to foreign policy the result would be chaotic. The politicians, as ever, must decide.

I believe the best method to arrive at a rational and defensible foreign policy is to start, rather as in the Australian White Paper discussed in the last chapter, by defining British interests on a country-by-country basis. At that level, though the difficulties do not entirely disappear, it is usually relatively easy to define where the national interest lies in promoting economic, commercial and security concerns as well as the observance of human rights, the protection of the environment and other goals. These assessments, collected and refined at the centre, provide a bedrock for policy. But they are not enough. Many issues are not country-specific and are increasingly transnational. So the British interest in the agenda of each multilateral organization must be similarly defined. Finally, probably the hardest task, the national interest in the looming 'new' issues – climate change, other environmental concerns, international crime, and so on – must be carefully assessed. This body of material will then underpin the more generalized statements of national interest which are necessary to mobilize support for policy and energize those who implement it. Such statements, unsupported by the groundwork I describe, will tend to lack conviction and sustainability.

The process of assessing British interests overseas is a major task, though in fact most of the material is readily available in papers routinely prepared by British overseas missions and by the Foreign Office and other Whitehall departments. A clear and persuasive description of national interest could only be produced by a detailed analysis of this material, which I have not undertaken. But I should be surprised if this methodology did not indicate clearly that the national interest requires, first and foremost, British membership of, and active engagement in, the European Union together with the maintenance of the closest possible relationship with the United States, where British economic interests are huge, our defence and intelligence interests are significant, and the benefits of attempting to enlist American power and leadership in support of our foreign policy aims are obvious. I believe it would also show that there is no region of the world in which we could cease diplomatic activity without unacceptable material damage or a sense of guilt that we had abandoned countries and peoples whom we had a duty to help. The assessment would justify constant effort to keep in good repair our bilateral relations with established key partners around the world outside the European Union – in Asia, the Middle East, Southern Africa, Eastern and

Central Europe and the Americas – as well as the development of relationships with newer partners of significance to Britain in, for example, Central Asia. The central importance of our involvement in the major multilateral organizations, especially the United Nations and NATO, would be clear. Our interest in playing a role in conflict-prevention and problem-solving as well as promoting democratic systems, good human rights' observance, relief of poverty and the freest possible markets would also emerge. I suspect, too, that the analysis would show that we need to organize ourselves more effectively to tackle the major transnational issues where conventional Whitehall techniques and diplomatic methods are probably inadequate.

The next step is to identify the assets which are available to pursue the national interest as defined. The assets directly under government control are obvious enough: political skills, the diplomatic service, with its extensive network of overseas posts, the armed forces and the resources of other Whitehall departments which are engaged internationally. The next category – not under state direction, but dependent on government financing and likely to pursue objectives which are consistent with government policy – embraces the British Council and the BBC World Service. Then there are a range of institutions and organizations which are independent of government but whose international influence and reputation for excellence are great strengths in the business of promoting Britain abroad. There are the best British firms, the City of London, the judiciary, the universities and other higher education institutions, the international non-governmental organizations based in London and national NGOs, to name but a few. Britain's international invest-ments are both a vital national interest and a source of British influence. Only America has a larger stock of foreign assets than Britain. The enduring popularity of Britain for investment by foreign firms is also a very sig-nificant element in Britain's international involvement. Finally, there are a group of assets which are less tangible. The world's use of the English language gives substantial advantages to British industry and to all British organiza-tions and individuals who work, live or are otherwise dependent upon abroad. That language, past and modern achievements in the arts and sciences, and the prominence of British media convey a powerful cultural image of Britain across the world.

We are rich in assets for the promotion of foreign policy. But while the government machine can seek to use them all in advancing our international objectives, most are independent of government direction. So, when interests and directly controlled assets have been identified, there is still the task of deciding how much government expendi-ture to devote to foreign policy and what objectives can be afforded and will be actively and seriously pursued as dis-tinct from being merely declaratory in nature. The proportion of government expenditure devoted to foreign policy in the broad sense has steadily shrunk over the years. It has done so as successive governments have sought to control and reduce public expenditure generally. As dis-cussed earlier, the methods of allocating funds to the various areas of government activity have in the past scarcely allowed a rational debate on how much should, in the national interest, be spent on overseas activities as opposed to other claims. To me it seems evident that, if Britain wishes to pursue an active policy abroad and maximize its interests, more needs to be spent in this area. A relatively small adjustment of resources would permit a fundamental shift in the effectiveness of foreign policy.

Beyond the assessment of interests and assets, and the arithmetic of resources, something more is needed. It has to do with 'vision', a way of describing objectives and activities which by its clarity and force gives them all meaning, not just for foreign policy practitioners but, more importantly, for the public at large and those foreign audiences who are in some way on the receiving end of policy. Vision is easily enough derided. You can get along without it. But however little political, business, sporting and other leaders use the word itself, the fact that they all seek to provide it through 'mission statements', manifestos and other devices strongly suggests that the concept is valuable. (I discovered a few years ago that even St Paul's Cathedral in London now has a mission statement, although one could be forgiven for thinking that its mission had been defined some time ago.)

In 1998 the American Secretary of State described the foreign policy goals of her country.[13] She argued that to protect national interests America must take action, forge agreements, create institutions and provide an example that would help bring the world closer together around the basic principles of democracy, open markets, the rule of law and a commitment to peace. Building such a world would require the United States to pass some rigorous tests. First, vision was needed, a conceptual framework that would tie the disparate strands of policy to interrelated core goals and set priorities so that the emphasis on responding to security threats, building a healthy world economy and promoting democracy was not lost in the blur of daily events. Then, pragmatism: was America getting results? 'Or are we so wrapped in how we sound that we forget that the purpose of public policy is not dialogue but deeds?' Third, spine: America must honour commitments, back words with actions, bear essential costs and take necessary risks. Fourth, resources: US foreign policy was today living hand-to-mouth. Last, the test of principle: how well did American actions live up to the country's ideals? The objectives set out in this text and the tests which were to be applied to American actions abroad provided overall guidelines for the conduct of the country's foreign policy.

In Britain, as seen earlier, outside observers searched in vain for a comparable statement in most of the post-war period. The archives are of course full of speeches by British leaders, some general in their thrust, some more specific. How far do recent speeches succeed in constructing an 'Idea of Britain' and of the British role abroad?

Some British foreign secretaries have preferred to let their approach to foreign policy-making emerge over time as they have dealt with and spoken about specific issues. Others have declared their general attitude at the outset. Shortly after he took up office in 1995, Malcolm Rifkind addressed the question of what the objectives of British foreign policy should be in the late twentieth century.[14] Quoting Palmerston's dictum that 'the furtherance of British interests should be the only object of a British foreign secretary', he defined these as our own territorial security and the maintenance of peace in Europe together with substantial and widespread interests around the globe which he described in some detail. Since those interests were so widely distributed and since we were major exporters and overseas investors we had a greater interest than others in political stability, freedom of trade and freedom of passage. We also had a moral and practical interest in promoting the values of liberal democracy. For all these reasons our foreign policy must be global in its application. In promoting our interests we should recognize that the nation-state was still the basic building-block of the international system but also that there were new global realities. The world was now less controllable, more interdependent. That did not make policy-making futile, but it did demand new approaches, accepting the limits on what governments can do by themselves and working within those limits and building alliances. We should not suppress national interests in order to construct an artificial consensus, a bogus unity. Influence was a means, not an end in itself. Occasionally it might be appropriate to accept a loss of influence if that was the only way to protect our interests.

We were committed members of the European Union but needed to revive the transatlantic partnership, principally by promoting the goal of transatlantic free trade. Getting the relationship with Europe and North America right was at the heart of a successful and effective British foreign policy. But we needed policy in the rest of the world as well. Admitting that his speech was far from a comprehensive survey, he nevertheless set out, among other things, the need for a new relationship with Russia, the development of relations with Central and Eastern Europe, more attention to the Pacific, closer engagement with South Asia, a new priority for Asia in general and more effort to exploit the 'priceless asset' of the Commonwealth. He concluded: 'Europe is being reborn . . . the world as a whole is drawing together to deal with global opportunities and global problems. Great Britain has both the power and the influence to make a significant contribution to that common effort. It is a national interest of the highest importance that we should succeed.'

In May 1997 Robin Cook, the Foreign Secretary of the new Labour government, issued a mission statement for the Foreign Office at a public ceremony in London: 'The mission of the Foreign and Commonwealth Office is to promote the national interests of the United Kingdom and to contribute to a strong world community.' Since subsequent debate chose to focus on what was commonly described as a 'new ethical foreign policy' it is useful to recall how the mission statement was developed in the rest of the text. Through our foreign policy four benefits would be pursued. The *security* of the United Kingdom and the Dependent Territories would be sought by promoting international stability, fostering our defence alliances and promoting arms control actively. *Prosperity* would be advanced by making maximum use of our overseas posts to promote trade abroad and boost jobs at home. To enhance the *quality of life*, we would work with others to protect the world's environment and counter the menace of drugs, terrorism and crime. To promote *mutual respect* we would work through international forums and bilateral relationships to spread the values of human rights, civil liberties and democracy which we demand for ourselves.

In attempting to secure these benefits for the United Kingdom, we would conduct a global foreign policy with five strategic aims over the five years of that Parliament – to make the UK a leading player in a Europe of independent nation-states; to strengthen the Commonwealth and improve the prosperity of, and co-operation between, its members; to use the status of the United Kingdom at the United Nations to secure more effective international action to keep the peace of the world and to combat poverty; to foster a people's diplomacy through services to British citizens abroad and by increasing respect and goodwill for Britain among the peoples of the world, drawing on the assets of the British Council and the BBC World Service; and to strengthen our relationships in all the world's regions. The statement concluded by listing immediate priorities for the year 1997/8. The text is printed in full in the Foreign Office's 1998 Annual Report to Parliament, where a more detailed description of objectives and the means of pursuing them is presented.[15]

The coherence and thrust of this statement were partly lost in the ensuing media debate which focused largely on the likely impact of importing ethical considerations into foreign policy-making. That discussion is not pursued here. A vignette may help to illustrate some of the inconsistency in the media coverage. As Permanent Under-Secretary at the time, I was invited by the Foreign Secretary to be present on the platform, together with all Foreign Office ministers, when the mission statement was launched. *The Economist* reported that 'Throughout the Press Conference, Sir John Coles looked like a man who had shown up for his customary lunch at the Athenaeum Club to find that it had been converted overnight into a heavy-leather-and-chains gay bar.'[16] By contrast, *The Independent* told its readers that I betrayed not a flicker of emotion throughout.[17] A recent book by another journalist notes that my contribution was 'to shuffle awkwardly',[18] which leads me to hope that the writer is still young enough not to be acquainted with the lower-back pain common to late middle age. For the record, I was closely consulted in the drafting of the statement. Whatever the individual views of officials it is their function to carry out ministerial policy at all times and most obviously after the election of a government with a fresh mandate. The general reaction of the Foreign Office, me included, was to welcome so clear a statement of objectives at the outset of a new government.

Naturally, since the two authors represented governments of different political complexions, there are clear differences between the 1995 and 1997 statements described above.[19] But it is worth noting some consistent threads. Both are firmly founded on the concept of national interest. Both emphasize the need for Britain's foreign policy to be global in reach and effect. Both focus on the security and prosperity of the United Kingdom as major priorities. Both emphasize the moral and practical interest in extending the values of liberal democracy. There are other similarities but these are perhaps sufficient to demonstrate a certain continuity in the concept of the British role overseas.

One last text. In November 1997 the Prime Minister spoke of the need for 'a clear definition of national purpose, not just what we want for Britain in itself, but the direction of the nation and how it deals with the outside world'.[20] Defining the key goals of national purpose – mostly domestic – Mr Blair included that of allowing 'Britain's standing in the world to grow and prosper'. We could not in these post-empire days be a superpower in the military sense but we could make Britain's presence in the world felt. 'With our historical alliances, we can be pivotal. We can be powerful in our influence – a nation to whom others listen,' on the assumption that we ran Britain well, had the right strategic alliances the world over and were engaged, open and intelligent in how we used them. We had valuable connections in the Commonwealth and in the English language. And we had many strengths:

> strong armed forces, a world-respected diplomatic service, international companies, the City, the British Council, the World Service, our global charities and NGOs. We have the technology and inventiveness. Most important, we have the people: entrepreneurs, creative talent in every field, world-renowned scientists, a dynamic multicultural, multi-ethnic society.

We had a unique set of relationships through the Security Council, NATO, the G8, Europe and the Commonwealth, and our close alliance with America. By virtue of our geography, our history and the strengths of our people, Britain was a global player.

Five 'guiding light' principles of a modern British foreign policy were described. First, we must be a leading player in Europe, where British national interests required us to be. Second, we should be strong in Europe *and* strong with the United States. There was no choice between the two. Third, we needed strong defence, not just to defend our country but for British influence abroad. Fourth, 'we [should] use power and influence for a purpose – for the values and aims we believe in'. Britain must be a key player on major transnational issues: the environment, drugs, terrorism, crime, human rights and development. Fifth, we must champion free trade and free investment.

Returning to the concept of national purpose, the Prime Minister stated that 'Foreign policy should not be seen as some self-contained part of government in a box marked "abroad" or "foreigners". It should complement and reflect our domestic goals. It should be part of our mission of national renewal.'

One way and another Britain does now have a statement of both the overriding purposes of its foreign policy and its detailed objectives, all in the public arena. The criticisms of the absence of those things described earlier in this book have not, I think, been adequately matched by recognition of their existence today. One reason for this is that the hard nut of presentation of foreign policy has not yet been decisively cracked. The specific objectives set out in annual departmental reports to Parliament, while publicly available, are not readily accessible to, and digestible by, the wider public. The appetite for foreign policy issues is small. The Prime Minister's speech summarized above received disappointingly little coverage of substance in the media. The fact is that serious coverage of foreign policy is hard to achieve in a world where the passion is for 'stories' of immediate appeal, preferably reducible to a sound-bite or two. The communications revolution obstructs rather than helps the communication of considered thought.

What to do? I have already argued the case for increased efforts to involve policy-thinking organizations and individuals from outside the machine and for the use of their ideas and experience in the process. But they might also be a principal target for dialogue about the outcome. I have advocated an annual White Paper on foreign policy which would describe and analyse recent achievements and setbacks, and set out future plans in a more digestible form than that provided by annual departmental reports. The White Paper would bring added value in that, conventionally, it would be a statement on behalf of the whole government, not the report of a single department, and would illustrate and promote the co-ordination of foreign policy across the whole of Whitehall. It would be a vehicle for more structured debate in both Houses of Parliament than now occurs in the rather thinly attended foreign affairs debates. It could provide a substantial focus for the work of the Select Committee on Foreign Affairs and perhaps other relevant Select Committees. It would then be valuable to engage the outside actors – business representatives, non-governmental organizations, think-tanks, academics and others – if not in its preparation, then in a structured and public discussion of its contents at, say, a regular annual conference. Even if media coverage was slight (and it might not be) a substantial audience of those most interested in foreign policy would be reached. Some flavour of the debate would filter down in their organizations. Material would be provided for further research, writing and debate on foreign policy issues.

I would like to think that more was possible. British activity abroad is extraordinarily rich and interesting. British forces in military action or in peace-keeping operations overseas provide images and stories every bit as stirring as some of the imperial adventures which captured the imagination of an older generation. British aid projects throughout the developing world often show British technical expertise and understanding of local conditions at their best. The bravery and dedication of field workers from charities and other non-governmental organizations in situations of desperate famine, disease and disorder are often compelling. The skill and courage of front-line journalists and photographers enrich the tapestry. The strength of the overseas impact of British culture and the attractive force of our educational institutions are crystal clear in very many lively British Council centres across the world in which you are nowadays most unlikely to meet Morris dancers but will encounter wide and diverse groups of mainly young foreigners, perhaps enjoying British literature, music and theatre but, just as likely, studying British science, management and design or completing applications for study visits to Britain or developing contacts in business and industry. The BBC World Service and World Television are listened to and watched in large cities and in remote rural areas. International devotees of the policy-making process have absorbed the diet of *Yes, Minister* for years in the most unlikely places. The familiarity with football teams and pop groups and fashion from this country among people who have no English and are never likely to visit Britain is often extraordinary. The whole story of British business enterprise the world over, active in markets established centuries ago and successfully breaking into new markets every day, is probably foreign to the average Briton. Immigration sections of British embassies and queues at British airports are potent evidence of the magnetism of this country for tourists, other visitors and would-be residents. The nine million or so British citizens who live abroad, and the three out of every five who travel overseas each year, put flesh on the statistics of overseas involvement. So, more coldly, do the figures of British nationals involved in emergency evacuation schemes or terrorist incidents or needing the assistance of British consular staff in other situations of personal distress. All over the world, at any given time, scores of British ministers, diplomats and other officials are involved in negotiating on behalf of British interests, a process far more absorbing than the eventual news clip claiming success or failure would suggest. Critics of the monarchy could usefully be exposed to the waves of popular enthusiasm which greet the Queen and other members of the royal family on their overseas visits. It is perfectly possible to derive from this huge variety of activity an enhanced satisfaction, and indeed pride, in what Britain achieves and offers abroad. But the picture is rarely, if ever, presented in anything like its full colour and variety. A part of what it means to be British is thereby lost.

The demise of Britishness is currently a fashionable theme. Devolution of government at home is seen by some as threatening the country's political integrity. Some fear that the steady integration of the European Union will eventually deprive the United Kingdom of economic and political decision-taking powers seen as essential to the constitution of a nation-state. The forces of globalization are, exaggeratedly, held to marginalize nation-states. No one can reliably forecast what the consequence of these trends will be for Britain's future status and power of action. But the debate is often conducted as though the strengths of the concept of Britishness do not exist or, at any rate, are destined quickly to fade. British activity overseas, and the foreign policy which in part guides and supports it, are only one demonstration, but an important one, that it is far too early to start preparing the wake. Some of us may think and hope that the wake will never be necessary. But for now, and certainly for a long time to come, the need for a British foreign policy, well-conceived and executed, and in the national interest, will be important to the idea of Britain.

EPILOGUE

I did not write the foregoing to attempt to justify some aspect or other of my diplomatic career. That would be boring enough for me and doubly so for readers. But there is a legitimate question: what did *you* do about the problems when you had the opportunity?

I tried to advance most of the solutions I have described in this book but some of the obstacles discussed got in the way. I attempted to convey to Foreign Office staff at home and abroad the message that the main object of our activity was good policy, that is to say policy designed to defend or advance British interests as defined by ministers. It was not enough to work for good relations with other countries and international organizations. They were worth having but were only a means to a larger end. I insisted on the right and duty of officials to submit advice to ministers even when the advice was likely to be unpalatable. It sometimes was, but no Foreign Secretary in my experience declined to consider it.

I took a strong interest in medium–term planning of

policy. I tried to give both the policy-planning staff and the policy advisory board (described earlier) the sense that their work was valuable but that their products had to be realistic and digestible. There were some successes. I recall several instances where medium-term policy advice led to new policy or modifications to existing policy. But it was a struggle. Any good planning paper, however concise, on a serious subject requires an hour or two of ministerial time if it is to be read carefully and its policy implications considered properly. But that ministerial time was hard to come by. I understood why. After dealing with a host of immediate issues in a late-night box any human being might find a weighty paper on a seemingly more remote issue, requiring complex thought, rather unwelcome. In theory weekends were available for reading of this kind but again the human factor might intervene: given the choice between yet more reading and an hour or two with the family or friends the first option would not automatically be chosen. I was never satisfied that we had properly engaged ministerial minds in medium-term policy thinking. That is one way in which the overload problem worked in practice.

There were some valuable strategic discussions with ministers but they were relatively few and far between. To have much chance of success they needed to be held away from London where the pressure of daily business could more easily be fended off. But often a day or half-day set aside for such discussion was lost because as the time approached some burning issue of the moment seemed more important. Potentially, the most valuable occasions were those when we brought back from abroad a group of heads of mission from a particular region or concerned with a particular issue. Such gatherings gave ministers the sense that they were dealing with the sharp end of policy but it was usually difficult for the Foreign Secretary to spend more than an hour, if that, with the assembled company.

The immediate preoccupations of foreign policy always loomed large. European affairs dominated the agenda but the public debate was so politically charged that it was often not easy to make the voice of officials heard. Bosnia provided a big challenge. For weeks at a time it was the issue uppermost in the minds of ministers. The transition process in Russia and Eastern and Central Europe needed continuous work. Hong Kong absorbed much time and energy as we approached the end of British administration in 1997. The variety and geographical spread of the issues we dealt with were impressive. The Foreign Office annual report for 1997 records more than a hundred achievements in the year 1995/6 but pretty well all of them were short-term in nature. As ever it was the day-to-day concerns that drove the agenda. There is no way round that.

Overload was always a problem and affected ministers and officials alike. Some of it was perhaps our own fault. Long working hours, pressure and flurry were part of Foreign Office culture. We liked to feel busy and under pressure. We wanted to be quicker than other countries in producing policy responses. We wanted our ministers to be the best briefed at international meetings. We were good at meeting deadlines. But it became necessary to question some of this culture. These things did not necessarily lead to good policy. Tired, pressurized officials were liable to make mistakes. The assault on excessive working hours began before I became Permanent Under-Secretary. I tried to continue it by vocally deploring the practice and setting an example myself. I made a habit of leaving my office at 6.45 p.m., partly so that no one could think that they would earn plaudits from me for working late. I would not know they had. Nor did they know that I worked in the car on the way home and often when I got there.

I suppose the biggest impediment to my efforts to improve the policy-making process was ministerial rotation. In the three years or so between August 1994 when I took over and November 1997 when I left there were three Foreign Secretaries, the last as a result of the 1997 general election. With each new one there is a settling-in period when he (always a he so far) has his own ideas to pursue and is engaged in mastering briefs on a raft of subjects and in establishing relationships in the international community. It is the period after that when it is reasonable to expect more strategic thinking but if the incumbent then changes again within a year or so the process cannot be taken very far.

I feel that I did make some progress in opening up the Foreign Office to outside expert opinion and to public opinion more generally. I strongly supported the 1995 public conference on Britain and the World described on

p. 156. I spent as much time as I could with business leaders, and in 1996 invited nearly two hundred major exporting companies to complete a detailed question- naire designed to elicit their thinking on the value of our work in supporting export promotion (with encouraging results). I established a practice of periodic working lunches with outside experts from industry, academia, the media and elsewhere to discuss privately a specific area of policy and assess its validity. As mentioned earlier I also invited leaders of non-governmental organizations to meet me and discuss our foreign policy objectives. In September 1997 we held an Open Day for 900 students, careers advisers and community leaders and later the same month received more than 15,000 members of the public who came to see the historic areas of the Foreign Office as part of the European Heritage Days scheme. In retrospect I think I should have done more to involve outside sources of advice and to promote public debate of foreign policy. My own efforts were too spasmodic. We needed a more regular system. (I understand that in the last couple of years the Foreign Office *has* developed a more regular dialogue with outsiders and has instituted a programme of recruitment of personnel to and from non-governmental organizations. That progress is much to be welcomed.)

I strengthened our machinery for dealing with transnational issues by setting up a global issues command. But I now believe that I should have done this earlier and, indeed, allocated more resources to this area of Foreign Office activity.

In two areas I was certainly unsuccessful. I made every effort in each annual spending round to obtain a real increase in the Foreign Office budget, convinced as I was that we were perilously close to being unable to provide the services that government, industry and the public required. I did not succeed. The budget continued to decline in real terms, reaching the point where, as discussed earlier, I do not believe the quality of services offered is sufficiently high, especially in the field of political analysis which is fundamental to nearly everything else. (In 1998, after I left, there *was* a small increase in the budget but I do not think it will be sufficient to solve the problem.) It is always difficult to prove that an international situation would have been better handled or an emergency evacuation of British subjects more safely conducted, that a business contract might have been won instead of lost or advice to British travellers would have been more reliable, had we had more expertise available in London and abroad. There will always be other explanations to hand. But having visited nearly all of the Foreign Office's seventy-four departments in London and having travelled far and wide to see the work of our overseas missions it is plain to me that there are many areas of weakness that need to be remedied. It is really a matter of common sense. If you keep cutting staff without cutting functions, sooner or later you are bound to reach the point where some of the functions are inadequately performed.

I did not succeed, either, in preventing management functions from eating into my policy responsibilities. Let me put some flesh on this problem. In 1995, in common with other Whitehall departments, we completed a Fundamental Expenditure Review designed to make our systems and organization more efficient, effective and economical in the pursuit of British interests and objectives. We were then required by the centre to carry out a Senior Management Review with the aim of devising the best possible structure for senior management in its task of delivering the functions and objectives set out in the Fundamental Expenditure Review. These two exercises were barely completed before we were asked to carry out a Comprehensive Spending Review, begun during my term of office but completed after I left. All these exercises, mundane as they may appear to most readers, involved a very large managerial effort on the part of many people. Since they were all designed to affect the systems and resources for the future conduct of foreign policy I was obliged to involve myself in them thoroughly. These and other reviews took many, many hours of my time.

Then there were the public aspects of management. I attended several hearings of the Select Committee on Foreign Affairs and the Public Accounts Committee which were related to various aspects of Foreign Office activity but only tangentially to policy. As a citizen I applaud this element in the democratic process. As the responsible official I was less enthusiastic, for these occasions required the most detailed preparation, taking perhaps the three weekends before each hearing. In public sessions lasting two hours or more the Committees expect, in answer to their questions, a pretty well complete mastery of often minute detail. No official takes these occasions lightly. Necessary as they are, they make large inroads into policy-thinking time. And these were just the special management events. There were plenty more routine management tasks to keep me going for most of the year.

I do not complain. It was absorbing work and much of it was essential. But I did feel that we had got our priorities wrong. We were trying to do too much of everything – and the casualty was policy.

I believe that if we had had more time and better mechanisms for strategic thinking, policy would have been better conceived. We would have addressed the fundamental issues arising from the disintegration of Yugoslavia more effectively. We would have had clearer policies towards Russia and Eastern and Central Europe where we were being outstripped by Germany and, to some extent, France. We would have adjusted policy and resources more quickly to the growing political and economic weight of Asia and pursued more vigorously the political and commercial opportunities provided by the process of reform which was changing so much of Latin America. If we could have found the resources we would have played a larger role in preventive diplomacy and the settlement of conflicts in the Middle East, Africa and elsewhere. I am less certain that we would have been more successful in developing a coherent and sustainable policy with respect to the European Union. This area of work was so intertwined with domestic issues and so politically delicate that it had become much more than a matter of foreign policy. But more strategic discussion might have helped. Certainly policy suffered from the absence of a coherent view of the desirable future nature of the Union and the role of Britain within it.

I doubt whether any comparable country could credibly claim more success for its foreign policy in these years and I still believe that our own was broadly successful. But it could have been, and still could be, better.

NOTES

PREFACE

1. Tony Blair, 'Speaking Mandarin', *Prospect*, December 1998.

CHAPTER 1: A CASE TO ANSWER?

1. P. Dunleavy, 'Policy Disasters: Explaining the UK's Record', *Public Policy and Administration*, Vol. 10, No. 2 (1995), pp. 52–70.
2. D. Butler, A. Adonis and T. Travers, *Failure in British Government: The Politics of the Poll Tax* (Oxford University Press, 1994), pp. 222–3.
3. Cited in D. Faulkner, 'Policy Making in the Home Office', in P. Barberis (ed.), *The Whitehall Reader: the UK's Administrative Machine in Action* (Open University Press, 1996), pp. 72–4.
4. Cited in P. Barberis, *The Elite of the Elite* (Dartmouth, 1996), pp. 213–14.
5. Peter Kemp, *Executive Agency Overview*, No. 6 (1996), p. 9.
6. Frank Cooper, 'Ministry of Defence' in J. Gretton and A. Harrison (eds.), *Reshaping Central Government* (Policy Journals, 1987), p. 125.
7. Peter Hennessy, *The Hidden Wiring: Unearthing the British Constitution* (Indigo, 1996), p. 165.

8. C. Foster and F. Plowden, *The State Under Stress* (Open University Press, 1996), pp. x and 220.

9. Percy Cradock, *In Pursuit of British Interests* (John Murray, 1997), p. 34.

10. Geoffrey Howe, *Conflict of Loyalty* (Pan Books, 1995), p. 568.

11. Peter Hennessy, *Cabinet* (Blackwell, 1986), p. 184.

12. Butler, Adonis and Travers, p. 196.

13. Andrew Marr, *Ruling Britannia* (Michael Joseph, 1995), pp. 273–4.

14. Howe, pp. 460–1.

15. Foster and Plowden, p. 212.

16. Foster and Plowden, p. 215.

17. M. Stuart, *Douglas Hurd: The Public Servant* (Mainstream, 1998), p. 329.

18. Magnus Linklater, *The Times*, 25 April 1996.

19. Peter Mandelson, 'Co-ordinating Government Policy', speech to Birmingham University conference on 'Modernizing the Policy Process', 16 September 1997.

20. Ferdinand Mount, *The British Constitution Now* (Mandarin, 1993), p. 129.

21. S. Pryce, *Presidentializing the Premiership* (Macmillan, 1997), p. 4.

22. A. Barnett, review of Pryce in *Times Literary Supplement*, 17 July 1998.

23. Foster and Plowden, pp. viii–x.

24. S. Richards, 'Promoting Change through Public Policy', Second Cantor Lecture on Creating Change, *RSA Journal*, April 1997.

25. Dunleavy, p. 62.

26. P. Hennessy, R. Hughes and J. Seaton, *Ready, Steady, Go! New Labour and Whitehall* (Fabian Society, April 1997).

27. Peter Hennessy, *The Essence of Public Service*, The 1997 John L. Manion Lecture (Canadian Centre for Management Development, 8 May 1997).

28. Marr, p. 341.

Notes

CHAPTER 2: FLOATING DOWNSTREAM?

1. Lady Gwendolen Cecil, *Life of the Marquis of Salisbury*, Vol. II, p. 130, cited in J. Frankel, *National Interest* (Pall Mall, 1970), p. 34.
2. See, for example, S. George, *Britain and European Integration since 1945* (Blackwell, 1991), pp. 34–5.
3. H. Young, *This Blessed Plot* (Macmillan, 1998), p. 32.
4. W. Wallace, 'Foreign Policy and National Identity in the United Kingdom', *International Affairs*, Vol. 67, No. 1, January 1991.
5. D. Brinkley, 'Dean Acheson and the Special Relationship', The West Point Speech, December 1962, *Historical Journal*, Vol. 33, No. 3, 1990.
6. Cited in P. Darby, *British Defence Policy East of Suez* (Oxford University Press, 1973), p. 22.
7. L. Martin and J. Garnett, *British Foreign Policy: Challenges and Choices of the 21st Century* (Chatham House Papers, 1997), p. 1.
8. See, for example, D. Saunders, *Losing an Empire, Finding a Role* (Macmillan, 1990).
9. R. Little, 'The Study of British Foreign Policy', in M. Smith, S. Smith and B. White (eds.), *British Foreign Policy: Tradition, Change and Transformation* (Unwin Hyman, 1988), pp. 251–7.
10. W. Wallace, 'British Foreign Policy after the Cold War', *International Affairs*, Vol. 63, No. 3, July 1992.
11. Wallace, 'British Foreign Policy'.
12. FO 371/188347, cited in Young, p. 190.
13. D. Allen, 'Britain and Western Europe', in Smith, Smith and White (eds.), p. 183.
14. Young, p. 245.
15. W. Wallace, *The Foreign Policy Process in Britain* (Royal Institute of International Affairs, 1975), p. 274.
16. See, for example, J.W. Young, *Britain and the World in the Twentieth Century* (Arnold, 1997).

17. Martin and Garnett, p. 14.
18. George Robertson, 'Britain in the New Europe', in *International Affairs*, 70th Anniversary issue (Royal Institute of International Affairs, October 1996).
19. P. Lawler, *Moral Vision and British Foreign Policy* (Manchester Papers in Politics, 1996), p. 1.
20. John Nott, *The Times*, 5 October 1987.
21. Lawler, p. 1.
22. Wallace, *The Foreign Policy Process*, p. 77.
23. J. Cable, 'Foreign Policy-making, Planning or Reflex?' in C. Hill and P. Beshoff (eds.), *Two Worlds of International Relations* (Routledge, 1994), pp. 108–9.
24. http://www.cabinetoffice.gov.uk/moderngov/1999/whitepaper/related/executive.htm.
25. M. Clarke, *British External Policy Making in the 1990s* (Macmillan, 1992), p. 111.
26. Hennessy, Hughes and Seaton, *Ready, Steady, Go!*
27. Cited in Cable, pp. 112–13.
28. Cited in Hennessy, *The Hidden Wiring*, p. 5.
29. Cited in Young, p. 34.
30. Peter Carrington, *Reflect on Things Past* (Fontana, 1989), p. 373.
31. Cradock, p. 22.
32. Cited in Clarke, p. 110.
33. William Strang, *The Diplomatic Career* (André Deutsch, 1962), p. 116.
34. Cable, p. 93.
35. D. Vital, *The Making of Foreign Policy* (Allen and Unwin, 1971), p. 111.
36. Hennessy, *The Hidden Wiring*, p. 171.
37. W. Wallace, 'Between Two Worlds: Think Tanks and Foreign Policy', in Hill and Beshoff (eds.), p. 148.
38. Foster and Plowden, p. 210.
39. See, for example, N. Myers, *Ultimate Security* (Island Press, 1996), p. 228.

40. David Owen, *Time to Declare* (Penguin, 1992), p. 354.

41. Cradock, pp. 97 and 186.

42. Both quotations cited in Young, p. 34.

43. Martin and Garnett, p. vii.

44. Zara Steiner (ed.), *The Times Survey of Foreign Ministries of the World* (Times Books, 1982), p. 28.

45. Timothy Garton-Ash, 'Germany's Choice', *Foreign Affairs*, Vol. 73, No. 4, July/August 1994.

46. 'Strengthening our Policy Capacity', Report of the Task Force on Strengthening the Policy Capacity of the Federal Government, 3 April 1995.

47. N. MacFarlane, 'The Emperor's New Clothes: Activism and Atrophy in Canadian Foreign Policy', lecture delivered at Lady Margaret Hall, Oxford, 29 October 1998.

48. See I.M. Destler, C.H. Gelb and A. Lake, *Our Own Worst Enemy: The Unmaking of American Foreign Policy* (Simon and Schuster, 1984), *passim*.

49. Cited in S. Hess, *Presidents and the Presidency* (Brookings Institution, Washington DC, 1996), pp. 64–5.

50. James R. Schlesinger, cited in Samuel P. Huntingdon, 'The Erosion of American National Interests', *Foreign Affairs*, Vol. 76, No. 5, September/October 1997.

51. Cited in Lawrence F. Kaplan, 'The Selling of American Foreign Policy', *Weekly Standard*, 28 April 1997.

CHAPTER 3: NOT FOR WANT OF TRYING

1. 'Proposals for Reform of the Foreign Service', Cmnd. 6420 (1943).

2. 'Stock-taking after VE Day', memorandum by Sir Orme Sargent, 11 July 1945, *Documents on British Policy Overseas (DBPO)*, Series 1, Vol. 1, No. 102.

3. 'Stocktaking II', memorandum by Gladwyn Jebb, 19 March 1947, FO Memoranda 5246.

Notes

4. 'Defence Policy and Global Strategy', reports by the Chief of Staff, 7 June 1950, *DBPO*, Series III, Vol. IV, Appendix 1; and 17 June 1952, Cabinet paper D. (52) 26.

5. *British Documents on the End of Empire (BDEE)*, Series A, Vol. III, No. 21.

6. *BDEE*, Series A, Vol. III, No. 21.

7. 'Defence: Outline of Future Policy', Cmnd. 124, April 1957.

8. GEN, 624/10, 9 June 1958 (CAB 130/139).

9. GEN, 659/1st Meeting (CAB 130/153).

10. C(60)35, 29 February 1960 (CAB 129/100).

11. R. Aldous and S. Lee (eds.), *Harold Macmillan and Britain's World Role* (Macmillan, 1996), p. 21.

12. 'Long-term Policies Group', Treasury document WP 7/4 (2211), June 1963.

13. 'Committee on Representational Services Overseas', Cmnd. 2276, February 1964.

14. 'Report of the Review Committee on Overseas Representation 1968/89' (The Duncan Report), Cmnd. 4107, July 1969.

15. 'Review of Overseas Representation: Report by the Central Policy Review Staff' (HMSO, 1977).

16. 'The United Kingdom's Overseas Representation', Cmnd. 7308.

17. *The Times*, 14 January 1993.

18. Stuart, pp. 395–6.

CHAPTER 4: ADVISERS AND DECIDERS

1. 'The Government's Expenditure Plans 1998–9', Cm. 3903, April 1998, Foreign and Commonwealth Office, pp. 2–3.

2. Cradock, p. 41.

3. Margaret Thatcher, *The Downing Street Years* (HarperCollins, 1993), p. 183.

4. Robin Cook, speech to One World Action seminar on 'Foreign Policy in the Twenty-First Century', London, 29 October 1997, *Report of Seminar* (One World Action, 1997).
5. Nik Gowing, *Media Coverage: Help or Hindrance in Conflict Prevention?* (Carnegie Corporation of New York, 1997), p. 25.
6. Cm. 3903.

CHAPTER 5: NOT WHAT IT WAS

1. Cm. 3903, pp. 82 and 91–3.
2. Marr, p. 7.
3. B. Crowe, 'Foreign Policy Making: Reflections of a Practitioner', *Government and Opposition*, Vol. 28, No. 2, Spring 1993.
4. M. Cox, *US Foreign Policy after the Cold War* (Royal Institute of International Affairs, 1995), p. 14.
5. Estimate by KPMG, quoted in *The Economist*, 23 January 1999.
6. Douglas Hurd, *The Search for Peace* (Little, Brown, 1997), p. 262.
7. R. Cooper, 'Irony and Foreign Policy', *Prospect*, December 1998.
8. 'The Myth of the Powerless State', *The Economist*, 7 October 1995.
9. Hurd, p. 128.

CHAPTER 6: PROBLEMS AND SOLUTIONS

1. D. Saunders and G. Edwards, 'Consensus and Diversity in Elite Opinion: The Views of the British Foreign Policy Elite', *Essex Papers in Politics in Government*, No. 94, 1992.
2. Marr, p. 15.
3. Hurd, p. 186.
4. Foreign Affairs Committee, 'Second Report: Sierra Leone', Vol. 1, 3 February 1999.

5. J. Dickie, *Inside the Foreign Office* (Chapmans, 1992), p. 317.
6. Cited by Lawrence Martin in 'Chatham House at 75', *International Affairs*, Vol. 71, No. 4, October 1995.
7. Letter to *Daily Telegraph*, 6 September 1989.
8. *Financial Times*, 21 October 1998.
9. *The Times*, 2 December 1998.
10. David Hannay, *The European Union's Common Foreign and Security Policy: A Menu for Reform* (Action Centre for Europe, 1996).
11. Foreword to E. Regelsberger, P. de Schoutheete and W. Wessels, *Foreign Policy of the European Union: From EPC to CFSP and Beyond* (Rienner, 1997).
12. R. Reeves, *What the People Know: Freedom and the Press* (Harvard University Press, 1998), pp. 3 and 88.
13. By Lord Lawson, cited in Hennessy, *The Hidden Wiring*, p. 110.
14. Hennessy, *The Hidden Wiring*, p. 114.
15. 'Consultation and Communications', *Public Management Occasional Papers No. 17* (OECD, 1997).
16. *Britain in the World*, 29 March 1995, conference proceedings published by the Royal Institute of International Affairs.
17. P. Unwin, *Hearts, Minds and Interests* (Profile Books, 1998), based on a study group established by the David Davies Memorial Institute of International Studies.
18. Cm. 3909, Annexes J and K.
19. The Civil Service Code, Cabinet Office, 1 January 1996.
20. Cited in the Civil Service Code, see note 19 above.
21. A new body, described in a speech by the Cabinet Secretary at the Islington Conference in October 1998.
22. A new unit in the Cabinet Office whose first projects were announced in December 1998.
23. 'Modernising Central Government', speech by the Rt. Hon. Tony Blair MP, October 1998.

Notes

Chapter 7: Australian Interlude

1. Gareth Evans, *Making Foreign Policy*, Australian Fabian Society pamphlet 60 (Canberra, 1989).
2. Gareth Evans, 'Australia's Regional Security', in G. Fry (ed.), *Australia's Regional Security* (Allen and Unwin, Sydney, 1991).
3. R. Garnaut, *Australia and the Northeast Asian Ascendancy* (Australian Government Publishing House, Canberra, 1989).
4. See, for example, J. Cotton and J. Ravenhill (eds.), *Seeking Asian Engagement: Australia in World Affairs, 1991–1995* (Oxford University Press, Melbourne, 1997).
5. G. Evans and B. Grant, *Australia's Foreign Relations in the World of the 1990s,* 2nd edition (Melbourne University Press, 1995).
6. Evans and Grant, p. 52.
7. Evans and Grant, p. 32.
8. Evans and Grant, p. 354.
9. 'In the National Interest: Australia's Foreign and Trade Policy', available on the Internet at http://www.dfat.gov.au/ini/wp.html.

Chapter 8: A Certain Idea of Britain

1. Charles de Gaulle, *War Memoirs*, trans. J. Griffin (Collins, 1995), Vol. 1, p. 9.
2. 'Report of the Review Committee on Overseas Representation 1968/69', Cmnd. 4107, July 1969.
3. 'Review of Overseas Representation: Report by the Central Policy Review Staff' (HMSO, 1977).
4. George Robertson, *Britain in the New Europe*, Royal Institute of International Affairs, Anniversary Issue, October 1990.
5. Douglas Hurd, debate on the Address, 17 November 1994.
6. Tony Blair, speech at Chatham House, 5 April 1995.
7. Unwin, p. 17.
8. S. Smith, 'Foreign Policy Analysis and the Study of British Foreign Policy', in L. Freedman and M. Clarke (eds.), *Britain in the World* (Cambridge University Press, 1991), p. 66.

9. Henry Kissinger, *Diplomacy* (Simon & Schuster, 1994), p. 109.

10. J. Frankel, *National Interest* (Macmillan, 1970), p. 24.

11. D. Souter, speech to One World Action seminar on 'Foreign Policy in the Twenty-first Century', London, 29 October 1997, *Report of Seminar* (One World Action, 1997).

12. Mary Kaldor, speech to One World Action seminar on 'Foreign Policy in the Twenty-first Century', London, 29 October 1997, *Report of Seminar* (One World Action, 1997).

13. Madeleine Albright, 'The Testing of American Foreign Policy', in *Foreign Affairs*, November/December 1998.

14. Malcolm Rifkind, speech at Chatham House, 21 September 1995.

15. Cm 3903.

16. *The Economist*, 17 May 1997.

17. *The Independent*, 13 May 1997.

18. J. Kampfner, *Robin Cook* (Gollancz, 1998), p. 133.

19. A comparison could also be made between Robin Cook's mission statement in the 1998 Foreign Office Annual Report and that by Malcolm Rifkind in the 1997 Report. I have, however, used the latter's 1995 speech as the point of comparison because it was made after taking office and had, perhaps, a more personal stamp.

20. No. 10 Press Statement, 'Prime Minister's Speech to the Lord Mayor's Banquet', 10 November 1997.

INDEX

Index

Britain (*continued*)
188, 190, 193, 197; national
interests and foreign policy, 180–6;
need for political information, 142;
overseas investments, 112, 185;
overseas role, 11, 181; overseas
views of, 143–5, 175–7, 185, 196–7;
permanent membership of UN
Security Council, 76, 97, 110, 142,
179–80, 193; policy mistakes and
successes in, 16–18, 28–9; political
and institutional qualities, 124–5;
post-war economic weakness, 62–5;
public expenditure reductions and
control, 185–6; recession (1987–8),
17; reduces imperial commitments,
42, 44; relations with USA and
Europe, 34–6, 38–41; status, 179–80
Britain and the World (Royal Institute
of International Affairs conference,
1995), 156, 201
British Broadcasting Corporation
(BBC): overseas role, 127, 144, 184,
190, 196
British Council: Berrill recommends
abolition or reorganization, 76;
function and activities, 144, 184,
190, 195–6; success, 127
Britishness: concept of, 197
Brittan, Sir Leon, 21
Brook, Sir Norman, 63, 65, 68
BSE ('mad cow disease'), 17–18, 141

Cabinet: and burden on ministers, 19;
committees on overseas affairs,
91–2; and European issues, 91–2;
and Macmillan's policy papers,
69–70; role in policy-making, 23,
30–1, 92, 152–3
Cabinet Office: Berrill recommends
new unit for overseas co-
ordination, 77; *see also* Central
Policy Review Staff; EDX
Cadogan, Sir Alexander, 53
Cairns Group, 165

Cambodia: Australian interest in, 166
Cameron Watt, Donald, 138
Canada: foreign policy-making, 56–7
Canadian International Development
Agency, 56
Caradon, Hugh Foot, Baron, 126
Carrington, Peter Carington, 6th
Baron, 48
Carter, Jimmy, 58
Central Asia, 148
Central Policy Review Staff (Cabinet
Office), 75
Centre for Management and Policy
Studies (Britain): established, 13, 161
CFSP *see* European Community:
Common Foreign and Security
Policy
Chequers: 1995 meeting on Britain's
overseas role, 79, 81
Child Support Agency, 16
China: 1984 agreement on Hong
Kong, 109; efforts to dominate, 66
Churchill, Sir Winston S.: on
preserving British power, 70; 'Three
Circles' concept, 34–7, 39, 82
civil liberties, 190
civil service: Berrill proposes merging
with Diplomatic Service, 77–8;
management reforms and practices,
26–7, 31–2, 158; policy advice, 16,
25–6, 32, 158; relation with
ministers, 158–60
Civil Service Code, 157
climate change, 113, 117, 182
Cold War: effect of end, 38–9, 47, 57,
112, 116
Coles, Sir John: described by media,
191
Committee on European Questions
(Cabinet), 91
Commonwealth: Berrill committee
recommendations on, 76; British
relations with, 34–6, 39, 189–90,
192–3; decline as object of interest,
82; Macmillan aims to strengthen, 69

Index

evacuations (of British abroad), 143,
147, 196
Evans, Gareth, 165, 167–9; *Australia's
Foreign Relations in the World of the
1990s*, 168

'failed states', 108, 115
Falklands: invasion and war (1982), 34,
52, 95
FCO Panel 2000, 144
force: use of, 114
forecasting and risk assessment, 138–41
Foreign and Commonwealth Office:
annual reports to Parliament, 103,
121, 156, 190, 194, 200; budget
limits, 203; and business interests,
97–8; changing image and
composition, 128–9; expenditure,
66, 204; geographical and
functional departments, 118–20,
147; hierarchical organization, 84,
87, 133–4; and human rights,
118–19; information from overseas
missions, 88–9; information sources,
102–3; lacks policy statements,
53–4; lacks strategic policy, 48–9;
management by objectives, 104–5;
management organization and
reform, 26–7, 31–2, 80, 106, 134–6,
159, 203–4; Mission Statements,
103–4, 189; News and Information
Departments, 86–7; opened to
public (September 1997), 202;
planning organization, 137–9;
Policy Advisory Board, 87–8, 199;
Policy Planning Staff, 87–8, 137,
199; political concerns, 142–3; and
presentation of Britain abroad,
144–5; prioritization and work
load, 130–3, 136–7, 141–2, 157;
process of policy-making, 84–106,
156–7; reaction to events, 50–1;
recruitment, 202; reformed under
Eden, 60; relations with other
government departments, 90–1, 97;
role of Permanent Secretary, 135;
social and economic concerns, 98,
113; suggested White Paper on
foreign policy, 156–7, 194; training
courses, 159; warns on Argentine
invasion of Falklands, 52; work
load, 200–1
foreign policy (British): assessment of
aims and effectiveness, 120–4; and
Britishness, 197; and business
interests, 97; lacks statements on
purpose, 54; process examined,
33–4, 83–106
Foreign Secretary: changes, 201;
relations with European Union,
95–6; role in policy-making, 93–4;
work load, 129–31
Foreign Service: amalgamated, 70;
formed under Eden, 60
Foster, Christopher and Francis
Plowden: *The State Under Stress*, 19
France: British post-war co-operation
with, 61; de Gaulle on idea of,
177–8; foreign policy-making, 55,
163; forms axis with Germany, 40;
policy on Eastern and Central
Europe, 205
Franks, Sir Oliver (*later* Baron), 37
free trade, 193
freedom of information, 160
Fundamental Expenditure Review
(1995), 80
'Future Policy Study, 1960–70' (paper,
1959), 68
'Future of the United Kingdom in
World Affairs' (memorandum,
1956), 63

G8 group, 93, 128, 179–80, 193
Garnaut Report (on Australia's
relations with NE Asia), 167
Gaulle, Charles de: *War Memoirs*, 177
Germany: British forces reduced in,
66; foreign policy goals, 55; foreign
policy-making machinery, 163;

Index